All In, All Yours

TYNDALE
MOMENTUM®

A Tyndale nonfiction imprint

A 100-Day Devotional Journey to
Find, Live, and Rest in God's Best

ALL IN, ALL YOURS

Heidi Lee Anderson

Visit Tyndale online at tyndale.com.

Visit Tyndale Momentum online at tyndalemomentum.com.

Visit the author online at heidileeandersonministries.com.

All In, All Yours: A 100-Day Devotional Journey to Find, Live, and Rest in God's Best

Cover design by Libby Dykstra

Interior design by Cathy Miller

Edited by Donna L. Berg

Published in association with the literary agency of Books & Such Literary Management, 52 Mission Circle, Suite 122, PMB 170, Santa Rosa, CA 95409.

For information about special discounts for bulk purchases, please contact Tyndale House Publishers at csresponse@tyndale.com, or call 1-855-277-9400.

ISBN 978-1-4964-7185-7

Printed in China

31 30 29 28 27 26 25
7 6 5 4 3 2 1

To the world's best parents, Dan and Robin Stoltz,
who showed me the Way from day one of my journey.

And to those uncertain of the next step in life, we're about to find that Siri, Alexa, and ChatGPT combined have NUTTIN' on God's living and active Word.

Best said in the voice of the famous theologian Dwight Schrute, "Let's get the party started!"

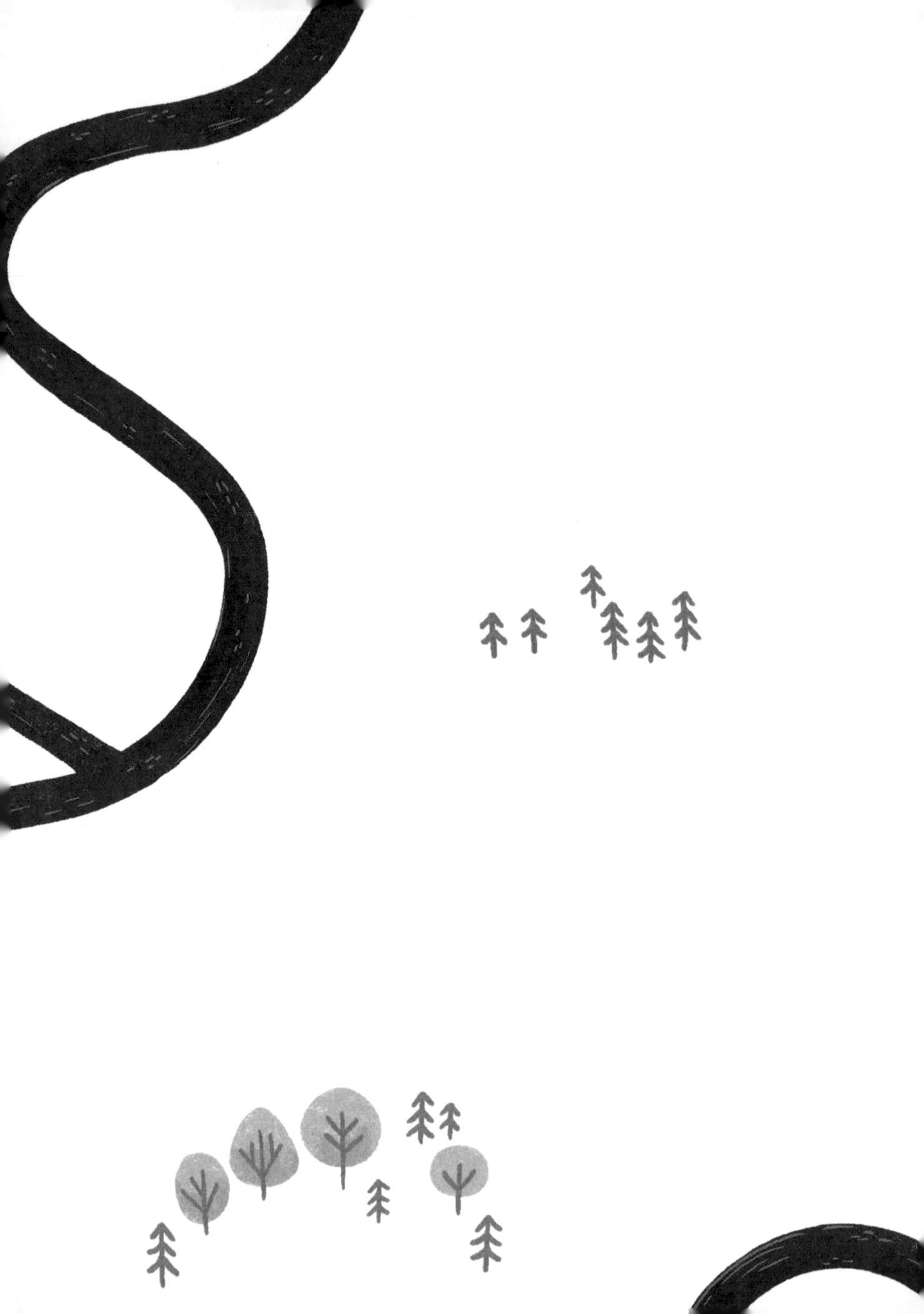

Contents

Let's Hit the Road, Jack— Er, Rather *(Insert Your Name Here)*

(But still sing along in your best Ray Charles voice, okay?)

. . . *Now what?*

You graduated from college, ready for the fresh start of adulting, but what job to take? Where to live? (And can we get an ETA on Mr. Right?)

You got married with high hopes of growing your family, but *how*, when pregnancy tests keep coming back negative month after month?

You've reached middle age, happy with life, but amid the mundane, you wrestle with your purpose and question, *Is there more?*

You land a dream job or hit a career high, but after this peak moment passes, what's next?

You're an empty nester with a quiet house, wondering what life even *is* without your kids and their activities?

Or you're retired, looking ahead at a new norm and asking, *How do I fill the time?*

Essentially, whichever stage you find yourself in, you're standing on the edge of the unknown without the GPS of life wondering, *Where do I go from here?*

Good news: You and I aren't the only ones to have asked that question. In fact, the Israelites beat us to it.

When we meet up with them, they are no longer wandering through the wilderness, killing time until their dreams come true. Finally standing on the brink of the Promised Land, they have at last been given the green light to move into their forever home, and we get to follow them inside. **FULL STEAM AHEAD, right?**

Wellllll, here's the deal: I don't want to spoil much, but it's important to note these people didn't just waltz into the Promised Land, call dibs on the first house they found, and roll out their welcome mats—happily ever after.

No.

Not only was there an overflowing river to cross (**in flood season, somehow without crocs?**). But like we'll see, there were also fortified walls they'd have to skirt past or scale without rock-climbing gear.

Did I mention there were current residents who were most definitely not interested in moving and considered themselves enemies of these Israelites (and oh yeah, were also GIANTS)?

Not counting family drama in full effect.

Safe to say there will be resistance. The question marks ahead will be scary. And the call to battle will go on (and on) for years.

But don't miss it: This strip of land was called the Promised Land because it was promised to them, and we in Christ are guaranteed our own territory as well.

With "the kingdom of God . . . in your midst" (Luke 17:21, NASB), we don't have to wait until heaven to experience it. We are given new life in Christ *this very second*. We are promised the free, abundant life in Him *today*. We get to dwell in His promises *presently*. We get to pray that His will would be done and that He would use us to bring heaven to this world *right now*.

But how?

Since the conquest of Canaan is one huge symbol of the Christian life, for the next one hundred days, let's follow the footsteps of the Israelites through their Promised Land to seize, thrive, and live in ours. No matter what stage of life you're in, you can still possess the land.

Here's how it's gonna work: There are ten mileposts throughout this journey with ten devotionals at each stretch. Daily, before we even take a step on our path, we'll first seek out our Guide, who is the Word, with a daily Scripture passage. Once we understand the lay of the land, we'll follow the trail set out for us through that day's devotional. To wrap up our daily hike, we'll answer a key question to help us take the next step through our own Promised Land. And get this—by the end of the journey, you will have traveled through the entire book of Joshua (*and some*). **HELLO, BIBLE SCHOLAR.**

But fair warning: The trek through the Promised Land is no easy jaunt. Beyond the change in elevation from valleys to mountainous terrain, I mean, we're talking 300,000 square miles. **(As an indoorsy person who's had altitude sickness more times than I can count, I'm already blowing in a bag.)**

Beyond that, there will be giants that resurrect from the past, a mission impossible that predates Tom Cruise, and more neighborhood drama than anything blowing up on Nextdoor.

We'll meet waters at flood stage, put our feet on the neck of evil kings, decipher tricky costumes that'll leave us puzzled about who's who, and team up with a pretty scandalous character.

I wish we had an app giving updates on real-time road conditions. It'd be amazing if Siri could let us know the quickest route. And what I wouldn't GIVE for Ubers to catch the first ride back when things start to go south. Worst part . . . there's definitely no DoorDash.

WE WILL LEGIT BE ROUGHIN' IT.

But even in the darkest of nights, when we're stressed over the next step, tired from the enemy's attacks, and losing sight of the promises, there's good news for us:

We already know the Way.

Jesus is the most faithful Guide, who will never leave us nor forsake us. And sure, while this is new terrain for *us*, He's gone before us and is familiar with every step we take.

What's more, He's the Light of the World—not just broadly for the whole earth, but specifically, as the Light of *your* world too. His Word is a lamp to your feet right now and a light to your path this very moment. "Even the darkness is not dark to you; the night is bright as the day" (Psalm 139:12, ESV).

As if we need more, He's also our Refuge and Fortress, our Strength and "place of safety," an "ever-present help in trouble" (Psalm 91:2; 46:1, NIV). Whenever you need Him, Jesus is only a prayer away. You can rest safely and soundly in His shadow and all-encompassing presence.

One last traveler's tip. It might be obvious. Maybe even more obvious than those "kitchen," "laundry," and "porch" farmhouse signs labeling every room in the house. But you must know the Promised Land was given with promise (Joshua 1:3-5, NIV):

- "I will give you every place where you set your foot."
- "Your territory will extend from the desert to Lebanon, and from the great river, the Euphrates—all the Hittite country—to the Mediterranean Sea in the west."
- "No one will be able to stand against you all the days of your life."
- "As I was with Moses, so I will be with you; I will never leave you nor forsake you."

Are you picking up what God's dropping down? The land is ours—with clear boundaries on every side to dispel any uncertainty. Enemies and trials lie ahead, sure, but victory is certain.

It's a done deal. Not just for the Israelites, but for us too.

As followers of Christ, we have been given the Land of Promise. "All of God's promises have been fulfilled in Christ with a resounding 'Yes!'" (2 Corinthians 1:20). Exactly like with the Israelites, He's given us the title to the territory that now in Christ rightfully belongs to us . . .

But like the Israelites, *we have to possess it* (Joshua 1:11).

This isn't a name-it-and-claim-it, false New Agey thing where if you visualize it and have enough faith, you got it!

No, this is a sound doctrine thing. It's a biblical principle we see from the Old Testament all the way to the New. This is absolute truth spoken by our good God who is faithful to His Word: He has given us a robust inheritance in Christ—but the responsibility falls on our shoulders to possess it. We don't claim what we want. *We claim His promises, which are more than we could ever want.*

This possession theme is repeated fifteen times in the book of Joshua—translating as "to occupy; to drive out previous tenants and take their place; to inherit,"[1] all as imperative verbs. No English major required. Do you see all the action? Alongside the promise of inheritance comes the charge to drive out and occupy. *As in, it's up to us how much of God's promises we'll believe, seize, and live in.*

He orders our steps, prepares the way, and carries out every promise on our behalf, but it's on us to actually place one foot in front of the other. God won't force us to obey and dwell in the land, but man, if we take Him up on His offer, we'll enjoy a lifetime supply of milk and honey, victory over every battle, progress and growth by His Spirit, peace amid the chaos, and ultimately, a closeness with God. You up for it?

"It is indeed a bountiful country. . . . But the people living there are powerful, and their towns are large and fortified. We even saw giants there. . . . They are stronger than we are! . . . [This land] will devour anyone who goes to live there" (Numbers 13:27-28, 31-32).

It may look bad at times, and if at any point you find yourself sitting on the edge of your seat with no idea how it's going to play out because you jumped into the sequel before the original, rest assured . . . *P.S. It's Gonna Be Good.*[2] **#hadto**

But trust me when I say, this is the trip of a lifetime.

So what do you say? I'm in if you are . . .

MILEPOST 1

Know What You're Stepping Into

Do you take time to read the instructions *before* assembling, cooking, or troubleshooting?

If so, what's that like? I never do. TBH, the side written in Chinese makes just as much sense as the flip side in English, so I usually fake it till I make it. Could be why I burn most meals and give up on assembling IKEA furniture halfway through . . . *could* be.

But here's the deal: Before Joshua even entered the land, God gave him an instruction manual. It wasn't an actual map that laid out exact next steps per se, but there were certain warnings to heed. Specific commands to ensure safety. And encouragement that would see Joshua through prior to entering the Promised Land.

We'll find these instructions still true and pretty important for us today too. Like Joshua, let's soak up every word, building a solid foundation for our conquest and gaining all the intel we need to know about what we're stepping into before we step into it.

Hmm, makes me wonder if those "read instructions before using" labels do hold some merit? Let's find out. You ready? All hands in on three.

One . . . two . . . three . . .

1

You Have the Deed to the Promise

Genesis 15:13, 16

When you look around the landscape of your life, what do you see? Maybe your season is early motherhood, and the baby is crying, the dirty diapers are fully ripe, and the rush of toddler demands is just ahead. Or maybe you're facing a challenging career, and the shadows of corporate giants are always looming. Or possibly after a big milestone with your health, your age, or your goals, you're looking ahead to uncharted territory, unsure what's behind that wall.

Before we barge into the Promised Land, we gotta look around at the landscape to know what we're stepping into. In the land surrounding Joshua and the Israelites, birds are chirping, acacia are in full bloom, and the rush of the Jordan River is just ahead. But so are the formidable walls of Jericho. The cities are already inhabited by many enemy nations (Exodus 33:2). And oh yeah, roaming lions and wild animals could "become too numerous for you" (Exodus 23:29, NASB).

So hold up. Why here of all places? Why have the Israelites set their sights on this chunk of land when it's already occupied? And excuse me, but what gives them the right to march in as if they own the place and push out people who have put down roots here for *centuries*?

Well, it's because they *do* own the place. Rewind to the beginning, and we find that when God blessed Abram as the father of many nations, He also gave him this exact plot of land as a permanent possession. "You can be sure that your descendants . . . will be oppressed as slaves for 400 years. . . . After four generations your descendants will return here to this land" (Genesis 15:13, 16).

Being those exact descendants four hundred years later, these Israelites are ready to march ahead. They are armed with the deed signed by the Creator of the land Himself, and you can almost hear them humming, determined to reclaim what rightfully belongs to them, "This land is my land . . . this land was [not] made for you and me." Without batting an eye, they are prepared to seize all that God has for them.

Like the Israelites, you have been armed with a promise from Jesus Himself: "The thief comes only to steal and kill and destroy; I came that they may have life and have it abundantly" (John 10:10, ESV).

This offer of life to the full isn't dependent on your circumstances. It doesn't change when the battle rages or the giants trespass. It doesn't dissolve when anxiety climbs to an all-time high, disappointment hits, or there are setbacks in your plans. No, this promise stands the test of time.

Yes, Jesus saved us for all eternity, giving us a heavenly home—and if that's all He ever did, that would be MORE than enough. **But our God is so good that He didn't stop there.**

Jesus also came to set us free *today* from sin, death, and shame. He sent His Spirit to dwell in us, bearing the fruit of love, joy, peace, patience, kindness, goodness, faithfulness, gentleness, and self-control (Galatians 5:22-23). He continually makes known the path of life to us. We are filled with joy in His presence and eternal pleasures at His right hand (Psalm 16:11). Each day, He is our Sun and our Shield, bestowing favor and honor, and withholding no good thing (Psalm 84:11). And He has "given you authority over all the power of the enemy. Nothing will injure you" (Luke 10:19).

Truly, with Him as our Good Shepherd, we "lack nothing" (Psalm 23:1, NIV). You have life . . . and in Christ, life to the *full* this very moment.

Like the Israelites, this is all the confidence you need for the road ahead: This land is your land. You hold the deed in hand. No matter what stands in the way, **it's time to move in.**

TAKE THE NEXT STEP

How can you view your circumstances today in light of being armed with the deed to God's promises?

2

You're Chosen for This Walk of Life

Joshua 1:1-2

Who is that person you look up to above anyone else?

(Besides Jesus, okay? I see your Sunday school answer, and I raise you to get creative.)

Maybe it's your parent—they love you unconditionally, have rarely led you astray, and their wisdom is downright heaven-sent.

Or maybe it's a leader in your industry—they took you under their wing and trained you on the ins and outs of the job, and their success is awe-inspiring.

Or maybe it's a friend who has overcome so much adversity, and their bravery, courage, and resilience are worthy of applause.

Ask the Israelites this same question, and they would've unanimously voted Moses.

Highlight reel: This guy busted them out of four-hundred-year-old chains, met with God face-to-face to record His law, and led His people toward the freedom of the Promised Land. Sprinkled between all of that, some of the most impressive miracles from God *we still talk about* were performed through his hand—including turning his staff into a serpent, changing the Nile to blood, creating a dry pathway through the Red Sea, and hitting a rock to burst forth a fountain of water.

God put it this way: "There has never been another prophet in Israel like Moses, whom the LORD knew face to face" (Deuteronomy 34:10).

So um, yeah. We can understand why Moses was held in high esteem, and we can also imagine the pressure Joshua feels. Big shoes to fill—wouldn't you, too, be intimidated?

But Joshua was chosen by God Himself to be Moses' successor. God straight-up said to Moses, "Take Joshua son of Nun, who has the Spirit in him, and lay your hands on him . . . publicly commission him to lead the people. Transfer some of your authority to him so the whole community of Israel will obey him" (Numbers 27:18-20).

In other words, Joshua won't be the same leader as Moses—because he is a completely different person—and he won't relate to God in the same face-to-face way his mentor did. But does that make him any less in the eyes of God or His people?

No. *Or at least, it shouldn't*. God has chosen Joshua and readied him for this particular time, and Joshua has the power of the Spirit living in him. Moses' leadership has been transferred to Joshua, and it is now on Joshua to roll up his sleeves and own it.

Wherever you feel pressure to live up to expectations, wherever you feel "less than" compared to others, and whatever has implanted insecurity in your mind, make no mistake: Like Joshua, you are chosen by God. You are sealed with the Holy Spirit. And He is sending you out to bring His Kingdom to earth. Refuse to compare. Cast off doubt in Jesus' name. And hear God's voice anew as He says to you, "Your time has come" (Joshua 1:2).

TAKE THE NEXT STEP

How do you need to walk forward with the same God-confidence Joshua had?

3

What's Defining You?

Joshua 1:1

Have you ever had something kind spoken over you?

Maybe it was from a coach who noticed your abilities, pushed you to the next level, and believed in your future. Maybe it was a teacher who showered you with encouragement and supported you every step of the way that school year. Or maybe it was a parent, grandparent, or friend who recognized what God put inside you, called it out, and with sweet words of affirmation, blessed you.

When I was going through chemotherapy, someone I barely knew at church came right up to me and said, "God is going to use your story to speak to the masses." Fast-forward to today, as I post about said story with an online community of hundreds of thousands of women . . . *well, how did she know?*

(Rhetorical, but just in case . . . God.)

As Joshua is standing on the brink of the Promised Land, it's important we rewind to Numbers 13, when Moses initially selected twelve leaders to go into Canaan and spy out the land. I'm picturing a scene like the Reaping in *The Hunger Games*—Moses drawing a name from the glass ball in the district of Ephraim, and the male tribute is chosen. With breath held, we hear who will participate: Hoshea son of Nun (Numbers 13:8).

Hold up, who's *Hoshea*? Skip to the bottom of the list, and we find the name change mentioned as if merely a sidenote: "Moses gave Hoshea son of Nun the name Joshua" (Numbers 13:16, NIV).

Here's the breakdown: While Hoshea means *salvation*, Joshua means *the Lord is salvation*.

Yes, Moses saw Joshua's natural ability to lead and raised him up to be his second-in-command. But Moses also knew deliverance could never rest on human shoulders. The Lord Almighty alone rescues, redeems, and liberates—and Moses declared that Joshua's life would showcase that.

This is true for us too.

God has put talents, skills, and spiritual gifts inside of you. He opens doors of opportunity you could never open on your own. And He calls you to step into them, doing "good works, which God prepared in advance for us to do" (Ephesians 2:10, NIV).

But if you rely on your own strength to get yourself across the sea, if you bank on your own competence to destroy your enemies, if you lean on your own intelligence to scale formidable walls, and if you trust in your own authority to settle in the Promised Land . . . well, no way you even get one foot in the door. More like washed up in the waves before you even begin!

Joshua knows this now—to the point that his name and entire identity are wrapped up in it. What about us? May Christ's salvation define who we are too.

TAKE THE NEXT STEP

How can you rest in God's ability to rescue, redeem, and liberate you instead of relying on your own strength?

Know today that Jesus hasn't just saved you from your *past* sin nor solely for your *future* with Him in eternity. As we stand on the cusp of the Promised Land, let's trust the Lord is *presently* our salvation too.

4

There's a Bigger Picture to the Puzzle

Joshua 1:1-3

Do you like puzzles?

No offense if you do . . . I (kinda) hate 'em. But my daughter finds them delightful, so every now and then, I get suckered into solving one.

Today's torture involved finding hidden items within the puzzle. You know, as if an additional challenge was needed. So there I sat, holding a piece that looked like a slice of pizza. About the time Hazel was nearly done with the entire puzzle, I finally solved that one mystery. The pepperonis were no mere circles of meat—they were polka dots . . . on the cone of a party hat.

Creative? 100 percent. What do I have to show for it? Nothing.

Here's what we need to know as we're piecing together the puzzle of the Promised Land: Each day, we're only holding one piece. It may look like a pizza today, and there's certainly enough cheese and pepperoni to chew on in every page. But it's also part of a greater picture, a grander purpose.

Take Joshua. Yesterday, we saw an assistant to Moses. Today, we see a man of God. Tomorrow, we'll look at the nation's new leader. But if we fast-forward 1,400 years, wanna know what else we'd spot? The second and greater Joshua: Jesus.

Lemme explain: The Bible is one book telling one story all pointing to one Person. All of it is "a shadow of the things that were to come; the reality, however, is found in Christ" (Colossians 2:17, NIV). As in, you can see Jesus in every book of the Bible, and with all the rich symbolism and deep metaphors, **no pizza is just a pizza**. If we piece together the puzzle, we'll find it's a party hat in the midst of a birthday celebration.

In particular, Joshua is categorized by scholars as a "type" of Christ, or a Jesus figure. Here are the similarities:

- Jesus and Joshua are the same name, Yehoshua—just in different languages. The Greek form translates as Jesus, whereas the Hebrew form translates as Joshua.[1] All three names mean "the Lord is salvation."
- While Joshua dedicated himself to the law of the Lord, Jesus perfectly kept the law *and* fulfilled it (Matthew 5:17-18).
- Where Joshua stood as a mediator between God and His people, making a covenant to serve God faithfully, Jesus is the one Mediator of a new covenant "who can reconcile God and humanity" (1 Timothy 2:5).
- As God used Joshua to bring the Israelites freedom and salvation from slavery, the Father made "Jesus, through his suffering, a perfect leader, fit to bring [people from all nations] into their salvation" (Hebrews 2:10) and out of the slavery of sin.
- While Joshua led Israel into the Promised Land overflowing with milk and honey, Jesus is leading us into the promised land of abundant life today and ultimately into our heavenly homeland (John 14:2-3; Revelation 21:1-4).
- Like Joshua led the victory over the Canaanites, Jesus leads us in victory over sin and death (1 Corinthians 15:57).

- Just as Joshua shared the inheritance with his people, Jesus deems us as joint heirs of His inheritance (Romans 8:17).
- Lastly, where Joshua gave the Israelites temporary rest from their enemies, Jesus gives a Sabbath rest for all eternity (Hebrews 4:9).

The same is true in your life. Yesterday, it may have looked like disaster. Today, it may be the picture of heartache. Tomorrow, it may seem like destruction. But your story ultimately points to Jesus too—and someday, those spicy pepperonis with their bitter black pepper will be transformed as we join in heaven's celebration. Bank on it: You will see for yourself how He fit all the puzzle pieces together for His glory and your good.

TAKE THE NEXT STEP

Which puzzle piece are you holding in your hand today? Can you see how it might fit into the bigger picture of God's purpose?

Before we claim the land and seize the victory, we've got to grab hold of this confidence that God will one day fit all the pieces together. Today, lift up your hands to Him in prayer (Psalm 63:4) and trust Him to move things into place when the time is right.

5

The Time Is Now

Joshua 1:2

"I'll be happy when ________________ is over." How would you fill in the blank?

Ever since I was diagnosed with cancer, there have always been milestones to celebrate:

- when blood tests showed improvement
- when tumors had shrunk
- when chemotherapy and radiation were complete
- when remission began

But mixed in with the rejoicing was still the hard:

- when clumps of hair fell out
- when the port in my chest made me feel like a robot
- when I was warned of infertility and sent to freeze my eggs
- when adverse effects hit—like screaming into a pillow when my tongue felt on fire

I thought that once I got that clean bill of health, I would be free. No longer burdened by biweekly tests. Unencumbered by daily trips to the radiation tube over lunch break. Ultimately, released from the death grip of cancer and the demons that came with it.

Yet for years, in between getting married and having babies, I was dragged back to recurring scans and annual appointments. While simultaneously cheering at my daughter's first steps and my son's first day of kindergarten, I was also holding my breath until results came back. As much as I was considered cancer-free, I didn't feel as untethered as I had hoped.

Yet I was told, by year ten, I could finally be free to live like a normal person. So I waited with great anticipation, prepared to celebrate.

But when the day finally came, I was shocked to hear the doctor say, "Congrats! You'll never have Hodgkin's lymphoma again. But now, we turn our eyes to secondary cancers, and these next five years, you run the highest risk of breast cancer. We're going to up your scans and reevaluate when you hit forty."

And then I realized. With the threat of heart failure in my forties and other diseases beyond that, there was no end to their timeline. There would always be tests to take, symptoms to keep an eye out for, risks to minimize. Essentially, there'd always be reasons to fear.

The same is true with *your* particular trials, and the same was true for the Israelites: "In this world you will have trouble" (John 16:33, NIV).

But what's also true is that even amid trouble, the time is *now* to seize what God has for us. "The time has come for you to lead these people . . . into the land I am giving them" (Joshua 1:2), and the time has also come for you to enter the Land of Promise—the free, abundant life in Christ.

We can't wait until our problems are gone to finally be happy, and we don't have the luxury of biding our time until the threat of all giants has passed to finally step into freedom. No, Jesus said, "If the Son sets you free, you are truly free" (John 8:36), and nothing you encounter can change that.

No more waiting. The moment has arrived, the hour is at hand, it's time to lay the past behind and seize all of what's been given to us in Christ today.

TAKE THE NEXT STEP

What milestone are you waiting for in order to be happy, feel free, or rest in Christ?

Surrender that circumstance to the Lord, and stand firm in the freedom that Christ already bought on your behalf.

6

In the Question Marks of Life

Joshua 1:3-4

Where do I go from here? In what area of life are you asking that question?

In parenthood? No matter what you do, your kid's behavior is just getting worse.

Your marriage? No amount of effort is melting the chill in your icy home.

Or just in general, the direction of your life? You were hoping to lead a life of purpose, but you don't know what that looks like. A certain job, a volunteer position, a concrete next step? Who knows? . . . Certainly not you. *(No offense.)*

As Joshua stands on the brink of the Promised Land, remember he's also grieving the loss of Moses, his mentor, his friend, and the nation's reverent leader. Not to mention having a horde of Israelites behind him, all awaiting his guidance. The questions must've been swirling around in his mind—with **Now what?** at the very top.

Good news for Joshua (and us): God doesn't leave His people hanging in the question marks of life. When we need help, He is our Helper (Psalm 115:9). When we need wisdom, He gives it generously (James 1:5). And when we're looking for our next move, He promises to determine and establish our steps (Proverbs 16:9), as he did for Joshua: "After the death of Moses . . . the LORD spoke to Joshua son of Nun, Moses' assistant. He said, . . . 'I promise you what I promised Moses: "Wherever you set foot, you will be on land I have given you. . . ." No one will be able to stand against you as long as you live. For I will be with you as I was with Moses. I will not fail you or abandon you'" (Joshua 1:1, 3, 5).

As you stand on the edge of your next season and unfamiliar landscape, you don't have to feel like God's left you in the dark, tripping your way through life. Rather, the Lord is speaking to you as well. Within 66 books, 1,189 chapters, and about 1,200 pages of His very Word, you have 5,467 divine promises to live in, any day, at any time.[2] As you crack open the Bible, you can be confident His Word is "living and active" and "a lamp to [your] feet and a light to [your] path" (Hebrews 4:12, ESV; Psalm 119:105, ESV), and bank everything on His Spirit to guide you.

Like Joshua, it won't be long until you see for yourself how "the LORD directs the steps of the godly. He delights in every detail of their lives. Though they stumble, they will never fall, for the LORD holds them by the hand" (Psalm 37:23-24).

But it starts with today. God took Joshua's hand, leading him toward and through the Promised Land, and you can trust this same faithful God to take hold of your right hand this very moment, reassuring you, "Do not fear; I will help you" (Isaiah 41:13, NIV). Instead of fretting over tomorrow, trust today's guidance is more than enough.

TAKE THE NEXT STEP

Fill in the blank: In light of ____________________, *now what?*

Instead of looking for concrete answers, look to the Lord. Seek His Kingdom first, and everything else will fall into place. God will faithfully guide you, and you have every reason to be excited instead of fearful.

7

Big Difference Between Feeling and Becoming

Joshua 1:6-9

Be honest: How many Christian cliché memorabilia do you own?

You know exactly what I'm talking about. That "Let go and let God" mug. The trendy "G>∧∨" sweatshirt. The "As for me and my house, we will serve the Lord" farmhouse sign. And we can't forget the "Too blessed to be stressed" bumper sticker.

What's your tally at?

I'll fess up first. My firstborn's life verse is the same as every Christian firstborn's life verse: "Have I not commanded you? Be strong and courageous. Do not be afraid; do not be discouraged, for the LORD your God will be with you wherever you go" (Joshua 1:9, NIV). So of course, we hung up a sign in his room the day he was born to remind him of this declaration day in and day out.

But here's the deal: This verse isn't just good inspiration for your **#mondaymotivation**. It's a direct command repeated three times back-to-back for Joshua as he approached the Land of Promise and then at least a dozen times in all of Scripture as well.

I mean, sure, we all *feel* fear at some point or another. But notice: God didn't tell Joshua, "Don't *feel* afraid." He just said don't *be*, and there's a big difference between what we're feeling and what we're becoming. This means, when we feel fear today, we have two options:

1. We can ride its roller coaster through every what-if, worst-case scenario, which then easily consumes us, dictates our actions, and spreads like a bad report throughout our mind and life.

OR

2. We can take that panicky thought captive and make it bow obediently to Christ (2 Corinthians 10:5) in a way that says, "Yeah, this giant IS huge, the walls ARE impossible to pass, the unknown IS daunting . . . but my God is with me, He is greater and bigger, and He still tells me I have no reason to be afraid or discouraged."

One pathway pushes us into the wilderness, away from our Promised Land, resigned to live in defeat and despair for the rest of our days. The other ushers us into the land overflowing with milk and honey, where we then bear witness to God defeating our giants, obliterating our obstacles, and establishing us in authority over our domain.

The next step is yours to take . . . Which pathway will you choose?

If you decide to listen to His voice and obey the command to stand strong and courageous, roll up your sleeves—because even if it sounds like a Christian cliché, mug and all, you'll get to see all of what God offers to you come to fruition in Christ.

TAKE THE NEXT STEP

Where is God calling you to be strong and courageous today?

Remember: How you *feel* doesn't have to determine what you become. For courage is not the absence of fear but "fear that has said its prayers"[3] and decidedly moves forward in faith.

8

Food for Thought

Joshua 1:8

What has your attention today? Is there something you're giving particular focus and effort to? Which way would you say this dominating focal point is steering your thoughts and actions—for better . . . or for worse?

I'll go first. As I write this, we're selling our house, and with an overwhelming list of to-dos before it goes on the market, it's crunch time. Learning to use a caulk gun, mulching the gardens, and painting the radiators has consumed my days—and my thoughts: *Will potential buyers value this? What kind of first impression does this make? Keep or ditch the original 1930s Mother Goose light switch covers?*

(We ditched . . . but DID WE MAKE A MISTAKE?)

In a way, being made in the image of our Creator, we're made to create—and I wonder if transforming a space delights us in a way that mirrors our Creator's delight when He turns ashes into beauty. My thoughts are being steered for the better then, no doubt!

On the other hand, when mounting pressures overpower that joy, and I find myself being impatient with my kids, worrying whether the house will sell, and obsessing over Mother Goose or matte black . . . well, it's clearly steering my thoughts for the worse.

All in all, what occupies our thoughts matters.

In Joshua 1:8, God tells Joshua to meditate on His Word day and night. Even though the word *meditate* has been redefined by yoga at the gym, a cross-legged Buddha lawn ornament, and a kung fu panda drop-kicking a snow leopard, the Creator of this world and the Originator of everything in it had a different plan in mind. He meant for us to contemplate His Word continually throughout our day. I know no better way to explain this than the way a cow chews on its cud.

Things are about to get weird, but stick with me. Just like a cow munches its meal while lying in the field, standing at the fence, or walking about, God wants us to chew on, ponder, and contemplate His Word whether we're sitting at home or walking along the road, when we lie down and when we get up (Deuteronomy 6:7).

But get this . . . once the cow swallows, it's not done. This disgusting creature regurgitates its meal . . . like, *on purpose*. It then gladly rechews it before swallowing again. ***green-faced throw-up emoji***

Don't miss this though. The cow is doing more than just vomiting (**and making us want to toss our own cookies too**). This animal is in fact extracting all of the nutrients possible and turning grass into creamy milk through this (very disturbing) process.[4]

SAY WHAAAAT?

I know. Like I said, *weird*. However, thanks to our undignified friends, can you now better see how God never intended for us to read Scripture as just another thing to check off our list and then move on to the next? Rather, Scripture is meant to set the foundation and undertone of our whole day. Like a cow chewing on feed and bringing it back up, we, too, should read God's Word, dwell on it, and keep recalling it all day long.

Not only does what we dwell on matter to God, but *how* we read it even matters to our success! God's instruction to Joshua is the same for us: "Study this Book of Instruction continually. Meditate on it day and night so you will be sure to obey everything written in it. Only then will you prosper and succeed in all you do" (Joshua 1:8).

TAKE THE NEXT STEP

How can you put this verse into practice and meditate on God's Word morning, noon, and night?

Let's trade the Mother Goose thoughts for the cud worth chewing over.

9

If God Says, "Jump," We Say, "How High?"

Joshua 1:7-8

Who are those people in your life who when they say, "Jump," you say, "How high?," not even thinking twice about it?

Your crunchy friend recommended cleaning products. *You immediately added to cart.*

Your parents shared their less-than-favorable opinion about a dating relationship. *You broke up with him.*

You thought your family was complete, but then your spouse suggested another baby would be nice. *Dottie came a year later.*

Oops, back to you . . .

Why is it you look to these people for advice, help, and wisdom?

Lemme answer my own question: It's because you trust them, right? Whether they've done the research, already lived through it, or are the experts, you realize they know more than you. And even more importantly, they care about you. Since they have your best interests at heart, you know they won't lead you astray.

All of the above is true about God:

- As the Creator of life, He knows the right way to live (Psalm 32:8).

- As One who is the Beginning and the End (Revelation 21:6) and has already gone before us (Deuteronomy 31:8), God has all experience under His belt.
- As the Architect of this world, He's the expert on how to build your house on the Rock (Matthew 7:24).
- Above all else, God cares about you so much that you, "out of all creation, became his prized possession" (James 1:18), and if truly "he did not spare even his own Son but gave him up for us all, won't he also give us everything else?" (Romans 8:32). As our Good Shepherd who dearly loves His sheep, He could never lead us astray and "is trustworthy in all he promises and faithful in all he does" (Psalm 145:13, NIV).

In light of this, what grounds do we have then to huff in annoyance or doubt God's reasoning when He gives a command? **Nada**.

When it finally clicks and we realize He wants and has what's best for us, that's when we drop everything like it's hot and "run in the path of [His] commands, for [He] has broadened [our] understanding" (Psalm 119:32, NIV).

This is exactly what Joshua does. He pairs God's instruction to meditate on this Book of Instruction day and night with God's warning, **given twice over**, to "be careful to obey all the instructions Moses gave you" (Joshua 1:7-8). And we gotta give him credit—from the beginning to the end of this book (**spoiler**), Joshua does obey. He knows there's reward in keeping God's commands and there's blessing in abiding in His will, *so he does.*

We, too, can spare ourselves from unnecessary conflict and heartache if we will only do the same. "What good is it, dear brothers and sisters, if you say you have faith but don't show it by your actions? . . . Unless it produces good deeds, it is dead and useless" (James 2:14, 17). Let's follow Joshua's footsteps, and not only meditate *but also obey.*

TAKE THE NEXT STEP

What is God commanding you to do today?

Let's echo the words of the psalmist and declare, "Open my eyes to see the wonderful truths in your instructions. . . . Make me walk along the path of your commands, for that is where my happiness is found. . . . For by them you give me life" (Psalm 119:18, 35, 93).

10

The #1 Reason to Be Strong and Courageous

Joshua 1:6-9

What's *your* biggest challenge currently? Let's name it. Is it a financial struggle? Personal loss of some sort? Issues within a specific relationship? Something to do with your health?

I'm gonna be honest. As I'm trying to meet the deadline for this book, we're also cleaning, painting, and renovating to get our house ready to sell, as I mentioned earlier. On top of that, my four kids are all home for summer break—and as much as I wish the environment was harmonious, **it looks more like real-life footage of *Mortal Kombat*. It's a challenge.**

Here's why I bring this up: All throughout the Bible, when God's people faced challenges, God showed up, repeating one specific truth and reassurance (italics added):

- As Jacob's on the run escaping his brother's wrath, God shows up in a dream saying, "*I am with you* and will watch over you wherever you go" (Genesis 28:15, NIV).
- Once David is established as king over Israel, the prophet Nathan relays God's words: "I took you from the pasture . . . and appointed you ruler over my people Israel. *I have been with you wherever you have gone*" (2 Samuel 7:8-9, NIV).

- As the Israelites are about to be thrown into seventy years of Babylonian captivity, Isaiah conveys God's promise, "Do not fear, for *I am with you*" (Isaiah 41:10, NIV).
- Immediately after Jesus gives His disciples the great commission to go out and make disciples of all nations, His final words are "Be sure of this: *I am with you always*" (Matthew 28:20).
- After Paul preaches the gospel to the Gentiles, is tried in court because of it, and everyone deserts him, he reports, "*The Lord stood at my side* and gave me strength" (2 Timothy 4:17, NIV).

Over and over and over again, God promises, *"I am with you."* So we shouldn't be surprised that God makes sure Joshua hears this too: "*I will be with you* as I was with Moses" (Joshua 1:5).

This was the fuel behind Joshua's strength and courage, and this is the whole reason you don't have to be afraid or discouraged either . . . "for the LORD your God *is with you* wherever you go" (Joshua 1:9).

Picture it today wherever you sit, stand, or go—**even and especially when the children are drop-kicking one another as if their lives depend on it**—God Himself is right next to you and goes with you.

TAKE THE NEXT STEP

To be *afraid* means to dread or fear. To be *dismayed* means to have your courage beaten or broken down. Where do you feel this today?

Whatever you're up against, this truth is yours for the taking: "If I go up to the heavens, you are there; if I make my bed in the depths, you are there. If I rise on the wings of the dawn, if I settle on the far side of the sea, even there your hand will guide me, your right hand will hold me fast" because "I am always with you; you hold me by my right hand" (Psalm 139:8-10, NIV; Psalm 73:23, NIV). *God is with you.*

THE FOUNDATION of your conquest

MILEPOST 2

Get Yo'self Ready

There are two types of people in this world: Those who do the research before vacations, and those who just show up to the researched vacations.

Which are you? I am . . . the latter, always stepping into what Ty has already laid out for me.

However, if like my husband, you thrive on googling attractions, comparing accommodations, and scoping out restaurants, then you fall in the same camp as Joshua. Instead of waltzing right into Canaan, he directed the people to pack and prepare, enlisted recruits to help, and sent out spies to inspect the land. Like we'll see, **homeboy did his homework**.

In the same respect, over these next ten days, we, too, will prepare as God is working behind the scenes. We'll team up with certain faith-filled men and women we can trust. And through our own investigations, we'll find salvation, protection, and the confidence we need to enter into the land **FOR REALS**.

Planners and nonplanners alike, roll up your sleeves because this is the good work. There are some things God has laid out for us since the beginning that we merely have to step into, but how we enter in matters to the overall success of the mission.

I'm with Larry the Cable Guy on this: **Let's get 'er done**.

11

The Win Is Yours, but You Still Gotta Armor Up

Joshua 1:10-11

What unknown are you facing?

Whenever we're entering a new beginning, a new place, or a new chapter of life, I get it. The possibilities may be downright exciting, but the challenges can be just as unnerving.

Yet it's key, especially when the undiscovered territory feels daunting, to remember we still always have two guarantees:

1. "Here on earth you will have many trials and sorrows . . ." **Yeah, yeah, yeah, that part (unfortunately) is true.**
2. **But good news for us: Jesus didn't end there.** In His very next breath, He declared, "But take heart, because I have overcome the world" (John 16:33).

For us as Christians, that's what every trial comes down to, and it's the perspective we need to keep. God never intends for us to stop halfway through His sentence, paralyzed by the trouble, taken down by the curve-balls of life. The enemy may aim for that, sure, but in Christ, he doesn't even have the power to do such a thing.

No, as we partner with God, He is faithful to "show Himself strong on behalf of those whose heart is loyal to Him," with the hope that we would be even further transformed into His image, going "from one degree of glory to another" (2 Chronicles 16:9, NKJV; 2 Corinthians 3:18, ESV).

Ultimately, every trial is only a test of faith, and God has set us up for the win. But in the meantime, we're still called to **armor up**.

With the Israelites, it was no different. The Lord had already assured Joshua that He had given them the Promised Land, their enemies would not stand against them, and He would never fail them.

But after this pep talk, what is the very next thing Joshua does? He tells the people, "Get your provisions ready. Three days from now you will cross the Jordan here to go in and take possession of the land the LORD your God is giving you for your own" (Joshua 1:10-11).

The victory was sure, but it wouldn't just fall into their laps. They needed to pack and prepare. They were charged to pick up their arms. And they were expected to march, fight, and seize.

In the same respect, despite all that we will face, "overwhelming victory is ours through Christ" (Romans 8:37). This ending is secure, but we still gotta suit up and "put on the full armor of God." Make no mistake, when we do and "the day of evil comes, you may be able to stand your ground" (Ephesians 6:13, NIV).

The trials may be guaranteed, but that is only part of the truth. Your victory in Christ is assured right along with them. Don't forget halfway through the promise: God will give you the means to stand up and *overcome*.

TAKE THE NEXT STEP

How are you being called to arm up and go out to battle today?

As easy as it is to get discouraged, remember that nothing this world or the enemy hurls your way can alter your happy ending. Heaven is your home, Jesus is your Bridegroom, He will win the day, and He "is able to . . . present you unblemished in His glorious presence, with great joy" (Jude 1:24, BSB).

12

Don't Settle

Joshua 1:12-15

Have you ever settled for less?

I'm talking about compromising. Where you once had preferences, standards, and desires, you began to make allowances. *Out of oat milk today? Okay, I'll sub almond. Not in my size? Well, it's on major sale, so I'll make it work! You don't want Mexican? Okay* (**you crazy**), *but let's grab Chinese takeout instead.*

On the one hand, this is just part of life. The theologians the Rolling Stones said it best: "You can't always get what you want." And it's good and necessary to be flexible (**or so says my husband** . . .).

But when it comes to major things, if we excuse certain behaviors, brush off warnings from loved ones, and finally accept our situation as is—even though it isn't the best (nor what we really wanted)—we're only robbing ourselves of a much better outcome. Like accepting a toxic work environment because you feel trapped or fear unemployment. Overlooking red flags in a relationship because no one is perfect and you love them. Going to a church merely out of obligation, for your parents' approval, or for religious tradition.

Or, as in the case of some of the Israelites, settling for land that wasn't the Promised Land.

Here's the context: While en route to Canaan, the Reubenites and

Gadites stopped in their tracks when they "saw that the lands of Jazer and Gilead were suitable for livestock" (Numbers 32:1, NIV). **Say (and see) no more!** Going straight to Moses, they pleaded, "Let this land be given to your servants as our possession. Do not make us cross the Jordan" (Numbers 32:5, NIV). Moses relented.

These two tribes were ready to settle because they couldn't fathom anything better than what was right before their eyes—and in the end, they convinced half the tribe of Manasseh to get in on the deal as well.

Are we, too, thinking we have a better plan than the one God has for us? Are we content to live outside the promise of God—settling for less than His very best?

Resisting change, prioritizing short-term fulfillment, and avoiding pain or conflict are always at the core of this decision. Echoing the Reubenites and Gadites' words, how would you fill in the blank? "Don't make me ____________."

There is a downside when we dwell outside of the promise. Reuben, Gad, and Manasseh "forfeited the natural protection of the Jordan River and left themselves susceptible to attacks from the east,"[1] and when the Assyrians later invade, these tribes "are the first ones to be taken because they are geographically closer to Assyria. . . . It is dangerous to live on the border."[2]

If we cling to what we think is best, we will miss *God's* best. Instead of settling, let's keep following Him **(and thus, being flexible)**—trusting He has "better things ahead than any we leave behind."[3]

TAKE THE NEXT STEP

Where might you be settling in your faith journey today?

Important: Don't stop on the east side of the Jordan, okay? Whatever you do, do not camp out on the fringe of Christianity, "do not give the devil a foothold" (Ephesians 4:27, NIV), and do not forfeit God's protection by living outside His will. You'll never regret crossing the river and coming into His fold.

13

The Three-Legged Race

Joshua 1:12-15

Do you like bike rides?

For years with little babies, I hung back, snailing along with a stroller while Ty and the older kids buzzed down the street, hair flapping in the wind, free as a bird.

Can you tell I was jealous?

But I will forever remember the year it all changed. We screwed on a copilot tagalong bike to the back of Ty's for Hazel and sprang for a toddler bike seat on the back of mine.

(Unsure why it took almost a decade and four kids to finally pay three dollars at a garage sale for this newfound freedom . . . but here we are.)

On our first few rides, I noticed Mabel, our oldest daughter, lagging behind on her bike. She would nervously slam on her brakes when cars drove by. She'd skittishly glance back as if her brother would (once again) rear-end her (**oops**). And she kept shouting, "Slow down!" even though we were already crawling like turtles.

Setting aside my fresh freedom, I spent several bike rides barely pedaling, determined to bring her up to speed.

Similarly, as God's people imagined the freedom that lay before them, Joshua called together the tribes of Reuben and Gad and the half-tribe of Manasseh for a group huddle.

These tribes had already been granted land outside of the Promised Land as their inheritance. Their wives, children, and livestock had settled there, rolled out their welcome mats, and started to put down roots.

But there was a clause to the agreement, and Joshua reminded the leaders of what they had signed up for: "Your strong warriors, fully armed, must lead the other tribes across the Jordan to help them conquer their territory. Stay with them until the LORD gives them rest, as he has given you rest, and until they, too, possess the land the LORD your God is giving them. Only then may you return and settle here" (Joshua 1:14-15).

Do you see it? These men had already overcome the enemies in *their* land. They were already basking in *their* rich inheritance. But they couldn't call it quits. They had a duty to see to their *brothers'* freedom as well.

We are no different. We may have taken Jesus up on His offer for the free, abundant life. We're dwelling in our inheritance as sons and daughters of the Almighty God, overcoming fiery darts aimed against us, and dwelling on the promises of God.

But just because *we* know the peace of God doesn't mean others do. So like these Israelite tribes, let's help our bro and sis conquer their territory too. Stay with them until the Lord gives them rest—just as He has given you rest. Support them until they possess the land the Lord is giving them—just as you have possessed your inheritance in Christ.

Why? Because we are first and foremost *family*.

TAKE THE NEXT STEP

Who can you come alongside to help or mentor in their faith?

"Be devoted to one another in love. Honor one another above yourselves" (Romans 12:10, NIV), and "bear one another's burdens, and so fulfill the law of Christ" (Galatians 6:2, ESV).

14

The Minority Is Greater than the Majority

Joshua 2:1

Are you good at keeping secrets?

There is one idea that always lands at the top of my husband's wish list for birthdays, Christmas, or Father's Day. While some would delight in grill tools or a beard grooming kit, I've got a man who wants nothing more than "any living animal."

You read that right.

So when his birthday rolled around, I hinted to the kids, "Guys, guess what we're giving Dad? A kitten! But *shh*, it's a surprise!" Aaaaand what does Mabel do? Immediately, as Ty walks down the stairs, she blurts, "Dad, we're getting you something you can pet!"

I looked at her in *exactly the way you're imagining*, and she evenly looked back, genuinely confused, and said, "What? I didn't tell him!"

On the cusp of the Promised Land, Moses sent twelve spies to survey the land, and what did they report? The majority claimed, "We can't attack those people. . . . The land we explored devours those living in it" (Numbers 13:31-32, NIV). Yet Caleb and Joshua pleaded, "Do not rebel against the LORD. And do not be afraid of the people of the land, because we will devour them. Their protection is gone, but the LORD is with us" (Numbers 14:9, NIV).

Who did Moses and all the Israelites listen to? Unfortunately, strength in numbers worked against Caleb and Joshua, and "*millions of people* were influenced by the opinions of only *10* fearful individuals."[4]

Fast-forward forty years, and Joshua stands in the same shoes as Moses. As tradition holds, his next step would be to send spies to scope out the land—but our guy knew better.

Fool me once, shame on you; fool me twice, shame on me.

Joshua knew all it would take was two faithful men of God to do the job. So instead of asking all of Israel for their opinions, he made the mission top secret, with the order that the spies were to report back to him—*and him alone.*

I'm a verbal processor and a recovering people pleaser. Without any filter, I'd blab my dreams, thoughts, and decisions to whoever I fancied—but then their hesitation, disapproval, or contradictions would trip me up. I'd go home, mulling over their words, allowing their doubts to increase mine. **Maybe this wasn't a good idea?**

With Joshua, we see it's okay to ask for wisdom. But it makes a difference who we confide in. In the original scouting report, not once did the majority mention God, but Caleb's account compared *everything* to God's promises. We, too, can team up with faithful men and women who pass every thought through this same filter: "What does God say about this in His Word?"

It's no secret: While other voices will convince you to bow out in fear, the Voice of truth will *always* call you to rise up in faith. Like Joshua, let's listen to Him above all else.

TAKE THE NEXT STEP

Who holds a place of influence in your life? Like Caleb's, is their advice founded in the wisdom of God's Word?

Just because more people agree with one stance doesn't make it true. Invest in a narrow group of spies who love God above all else, and just watch how your plans succeed.

15

Your Fears Are Not Terrifying . . . They're the Ones Terrified

Joshua 2:8-24

What's your deepest, darkest, biggest fear of all time?

If nothing pops into your mind (#bless), maybe the top ten most common fears might strike a chord?

- public speaking
- heights
- going to the dentist
- snakes
- flying
- spiders and insects
- enclosed spaces or darkness
- death or dying
- failure or rejection
- germs or developing a disease

The Israelites' top fear didn't make our modern-day list, but maybe those of us who believe Sasquatch to be more fact, less folklore can resonate . . .

Canaanite giants.

Their size was unmatched. Their military strength was renowned. And their fortressed cities were impenetrable.

In light of these towering enemies, who were the Israelites but mere grasshoppers? They certainly thought so themselves—"We can't attack those people; they are stronger than we are" (Numbers 13:31, NIV)—and in the end, they chose to believe their fear was bigger than their God—*and paid the price.*

Fast-forward forty years to Joshua 2, when God gives the green light to enter the Promised Land. Joshua sends out two spies, and one important, specific emotion is repeated four times in this chapter alone. See if you pick up on it:

> [Rahab said to the spies], "I know that the LORD has given you this land and that a great fear of you has fallen on us, so that all who live in this country are melting in fear because of you. . . . When we heard of [the miraculous works of God], our hearts melted in fear and everyone's courage failed because of you. . . ." [Reporting back to camp], they said to Joshua, "The LORD has surely given the whole land into our hands; all the people are melting in fear because of us."
>
> JOSHUA 2:9, 11, 24, NIV

Like chocolate melting in the hands of a toddler, these terrifying Canaanites were actually terrified of *the Israelites*—or more accurately, of the God who stood with them.

This isn't just a one-off thing. Flip over to the New Testament, and when Jesus sets foot into enemy-held territory, the demons shout, "What do you want with us, Son of God? . . . Have you come here to torture us before the appointed time?" (Matthew 8:29, NIV).

Don't miss it: These violent demons, who caused everyone to cower, bowed to whom?

Jesus.

As former angels, of course they knew exactly who He was. They called Jesus the Son of God—acknowledging that He's "the radiance of God's glory and the exact representation of his being, sustaining all things by his powerful word" (Hebrews 1:3, NIV).

What's more, they knew their future appointment: "the eternal fire prepared for the devil and his demons" (Matthew 25:41). Recognizing Jesus' authority over them, they begged for another destination: "If you cast us out, send us into that herd of pigs" (Matthew 8:31).

Here's the point: All too often, we feel our fears are bigger than we are, holding the upper hand. But it's of dire importance that we remember who is greater than any other and *is living within us*: **the Son of God**. Make no mistake: Our fears are rightfully terrified of *Him*. Do we hold this same, right perspective?

TAKE THE NEXT STEP

In what way is your heart melting in fear today?

Very few Canaanites turned to peace, but Rahab did—and we can too. Whatever you're facing, remember who stands with you . . . He is greater, and He is your peace.

16

What's Your Jericho?

Joshua 2:1

Let's get all sentimental for a sec and reminisce about your childhood.

Usually, I'd love to hear about those memories that give you all the fuzzies, but . . . can I pry a bit? Is there a bad habit, a negative attitude, or a painful experience that still filters into your thought life today?

I know, a little bold, kinda Negative Nancy—but maybe there was explosive anger in your home. Or a complete disregard for God that you battle even now. Or possibly it was the careless words of a classmate, that scary diagnosis for a loved one, or a trusted adult turned negligent that chipped away at your confidence, hope, and spirit.

I only ask because when Joshua sent out his two trusty spies into the Promised Land, he specifically commanded, "Scout out the land on the other side of the Jordan River, *especially around Jericho*" (Joshua 2:1, italics added).

Why Jericho? Why was it such a point of interest?

Well, for one thing, these Israelites were camped in Shittim, only fourteen miles away. Jericho was the closest entrance into the land—logically, the next step.

But for another, it was a flourishing oasis and one of the oldest cities in civilization, "occupied and fortified since *c.* 7000 BC."[5]

Lastly, with its tall walls and towering fortification, it allowed Israel to secure a strong foothold in claiming the land.[6]

Do you see what I'm seeing? Joshua was being strategic, and in the same way, *we* must be strategic about which stronghold we attack first in our own lives.

There are old lies we have been believing since childhood—*I'm not good enough, I have to be perfect, God isn't trustworthy, I have license to lash out at whomever I want, God won't protect me.* Like the long-established Jericho, they've been embedded in our minds for so long that we've become familiar with their regular whisper. But it's a dangerous thing to keep drinking from this contaminated well. Rather than giving life, these lies only produce death, and they give the enemy a foothold.

While it may also seem impossible to tear down their thick walls, remember: "The weapons we fight with . . . have divine power to demolish strongholds" (2 Corinthians 10:4, NIV). To demolish means "to destroy or ruin . . . *especially on purpose*" (italics added).[7]

So what do you say? Our God is the very Chain Breaker who "bursts [our] bonds apart" (Psalm 107:14, ESV)—and He's ready to free you once and for all. But these marching orders require intention, and our attack will have to be deliberate. Yet make no mistake, if you take this step, you'll gain a major foothold in the Land of Promise. Yeah, you look ready to me. **It's time for Jericho to go.**

TAKE THE NEXT STEP

What's your Jericho?

God doesn't want you to tolerate it a moment longer, letting it wreak havoc in your life. In the powerful name of Jesus, it's time to bulldoze that sucker to the ground, so go forth with full reassurance: "If God is for us, who can ever be against us?" (Romans 8:31).

17

He's Preparing What He's Prepared for You

Joshua 2:1

Are you waiting around for something?

Waiting for that dream to come true, to start a family, or for your spouse to show some warmth? Waiting to feel better, to figure out next steps, and to finally get some answers? Waiting for peace, financial security, a good job offer, or healing in a friendship?

For years, I've struggled with heartburn and acid reflux, and it seems to come and go without warning. I've recently had a bad flare-up that resulted in scary chest pain. On top of that, a blood panel showed my cholesterol was high. With my oncologist's warning of future heart concerns, my mind has been on high alert.

Wanna know what the suggestions are to bring relief and lower my count? Exercise. Cut sugar. Don't smoke or drink alcohol. Avoid eating at night. Eat a GERD-friendly diet. Reduce stress.

Listen. I've already been working out at least five times a week. I've been off sugar for a couple years. I've never smoked or drank. I cut out late-night snacks long ago. I feel like a rabbit with my vegetable consumption.

And stress? Well, after I mashed an avocado, marinated black beans in a homemade taco seasoning, and waited for my lame sweet potato to bake, our cat helped himself to my meal . . . *and I lost it.* I broke down in tears and sank onto my bed with palms raised, asking, "God, how long until you heal me? **(And please don't let the answer be when I give up** ***coffee*** **. . .)**"

Related: While Joshua's two men were spying out the Promised Land, let's pan back to our Israelite friends. What were they doing during this time of waiting?

Remember, the spies were on a *covert* mission. As in, their Canaanite enemies were unaware, and it seems their brothers and sisters back in Shittim were uninformed as well. They were told to wait around for three days getting ready—but unbeknownst to them, God was strategically setting up their path through the Promised Land, and this concealed work by the chosen scouts was important for their future success and progress.

The same is true for us. While we can only see some things, God sees all things—and with Him who never slumbers or takes time off from watching over us, we can trust He is moving, *even and especially when we're waiting.* Jesus said, "My Father is always at his work to this very day, and I too am working" (John 15:17, NIV).

Lemme repeat: God is always, constantly, every minute and each second of our every day, at work.

We may not have been involved in the strategic planning meeting.

We may be completely clueless as to what's happening across the river.

We may be feeling like it's just time wasted, begging God to tell us, *What's the next step? Where's the help? When will the breakthrough come?*

Take heart today knowing that God is on the move. Just like there was a special purpose in the Israelites' waiting, there is a good reason God has you where He does today too.

So sit tight and "humble yourselves, therefore, under God's mighty hand, that he may lift you up in due time" (1 Peter 5:6). The right time *is* coming. We need only to wait on Him.

TAKE THE NEXT STEP

How do you resonate with the rest of the Israelite army?

Shift your perspective to realize you're not waiting aimlessly, but that our God is and will always be bringing about a good purpose.

18

I'll Believe It When I See It . . . or I'll See It When I Believe It?

Joshua 2:1-11

Ever thought, "I'll believe it when I see it"?

Your kids tell you they'll clean their room later . . . **like today or in fifty years?** The weather app warns of a storm brewing with nothing but clear skies outside . . . **suuure**. A certain spacey friend promises to pay you back . . . **like last time?**

Yeah, I'm gonna need TANGIBLE EVIDENCE to believe a lick of any of that.

Thomas felt the same way. After Jesus was resurrected from the dead, they jumped up and down to tell Tommy Boy the news: "We have seen the Lord!" But he just blinked back at them. "I won't believe it unless I see the nail wounds in his hands, put my fingers into them, and place my hand into the wound in his side" (John 20:25).

But seeing isn't always believing, is it?

God parted the Red Sea and destroyed the Amorite kings for His people, yet that generation of Israelites? They believed the fortifications of man were greater than the power of God . . . and for the remainder of their lives, wandered in the wilderness.

But as the spies creep into enemy-held territory and hide in the home of a Canaanite prostitute named Rahab, what do we hear coming from her lips? "We have heard how the LORD made a dry path for you through the Red Sea when you left Egypt. And we know what you did to Sihon and Og, the two Amorite kings east of the Jordan River, whose people you completely destroyed . . . No one has the courage to fight after hearing such things. For the LORD your God is the supreme God" (Joshua 2:10-11).

We can't miss this: When she says, "I know the LORD has given you this land" (Joshua 2:9), the Hebrew word used for "know" is *yada*—which means a kind of knowledge based in conviction, not simply familiarity.[8] Not to mention, the term "LORD" she uses with such confidence is God's personal name, the Hebrew covenant name for God: Yahweh.[9]

As in, Rahab has given her full allegiance to God alone. The Israelites who had been eyewitnesses to God's miracles didn't even hold this kind of faith—a faith that was so convinced of His rule over superpower leaders and His power over impassable walls and fully armed enemies. But based merely on hearsay, Rahab believed, because "faith comes from hearing the message" (Romans 10:17, NIV).

Hundreds of years later, after relentless crowds had badgered Jesus for a miracle, He stood before Thomas and said, "You believe because you have seen me. Blessed are those who believe without seeing me" (John 20:29).

BTW that's you. Or at least, it *can* be you. You may not have seen the answered prayers, the miracles, or the Bible stories with your own eyes. But you, too, can believe, and it won't be long until your eyes are opened to the ways God has been moving all along, declaring "My ears had heard of you, but now my eyes have seen you" (Job 42:5).

TAKE THE NEXT STEP

In what ways do you resonate with Rahab?

Let's echo her words and focus on the sovereignty of God: "The LORD [my] God is the supreme God of the heavens above and the earth below" (Joshua 2:11).

19

Enter While the Door Is Open

Joshua 2:12-21

Where do you go when life feels like a battle?

Is it to your parents? **Do you, too, beeline straight to your spouse or your parents?** What about Netflix for comedic relief or a good book to get lost in someone else's life? Or do you go straight to the fridge? Spin dip, a chunk of cheese, ice cream, doesn't matter—**even expired chips start to look appealing when we're trying to eat our problems, you know?**

Rewind to Egypt, right before God busted His people out of slavery and led them into freedom. It was the night of Passover. Each household splashed blood from an unblemished lamb across their doorframes—not as eccentric curb appeal, but as a sign directed by God Himself: "When I see the blood, I will pass over you. No destructive plague will touch you when I strike Egypt" (Exodus 12:13, NIV).

Now jog back to Joshua 2, and how does the conversation between Rahab and the hidden spies go down? Like a woman who won't take no for an answer, she demands, "Give me some guarantee that when Jericho is conquered, you will let me live, along with my father and mother, my brothers and sisters, and all their families" (Joshua 2:12-13). **Go for broke, girl!**

The spies' response? Hang the very scarlet rope lowered for their escape out the same window, so when they seize Jericho, destruction would pass over, keeping those inside safe.

Sense a theme? Good, because just a hop, skip, and jump away in the New Testament, as scarlet blood pours forth from the Lamb of God, we realize what these earlier stories had been pointing to all along: "In him we have redemption through his blood, the forgiveness of sins, in accordance with the riches of God's grace that he lavished on us" (Ephesians 1:7-8, NIV).

Where there was no scarlet covering, there was death. But anyone who entered in and placed their trust in God's salvation certainly found safety and life abundant.

This is true today too. No matter the chaos outside your doors, know you can follow Rahab's footsteps and "take refuge in the shadow of [His] wings until the disaster has passed" (Psalm 57:1, NIV). Every other part of the fortressed city was laid flat, but the little alcove of Rahab's abode miraculously remained standing. **God offers you the same covering.**

Truly, Jesus is the Gate and "whoever enters through [him] will be saved" (John 10:9, NIV). Even if others don't take Him up on His invitation, Jesus has given His life for you, and by His blood, you can be made right in God's sight, saved from condemnation, *today* (Romans 5:9). What do you say we enter in while the Door is still open?

TAKE THE NEXT STEP

What war is currently being waged around you?

Enter the Gate and put yourself under the protection of the Almighty. It really is a matter of life and death—figuratively and literally—so come on in and rest soundly, knowing "after the battle, you will still be standing firm" (Ephesians 6:13), protected under His wing and His armor.

20

Your Before-and-After Story

Joshua 2:1-24

Do you love a good before-and-after story as much as I do? It stops my scroll every time. Reels where someone chops their long locks to just above their shoulders or a photographer shows their raw image next to their edited one. Not to mention the house flips or the moms who turn their disastrous living rooms into clean perfection just by sneezing into their arms! **About that last one . . . INQUIRING MINDS WOULD LIKE TO KNOW *HOW*.**

We may not make a reel about it or have pictures to prove it, but you and I have our own before-and-after story—just like Rahab.

Before, she was a prostitute who lived as an outcast literally on the outskirts of town, "her home built into the town wall" (Joshua 2:15). Plus, she was a Canaanite, which made her the hated enemy of Israel, and she was a citizen of Jericho—aka the Moon City because those inside its walls practiced lunar worship.[10]

But *after* she heard the report of the Lord drying up the Red Sea for His people, and *after* she learned that the Israelites had destroyed the Amorite kings so famous for their strength and power? Well, Rahab reasonably deduced, "The Lord your God is the supreme God of the heavens above and the earth below" (Joshua 2:11).

Rahab is mentioned in eight passages of Scripture though, and her name is often paired with a specific descriptive noun—*harlot*. While she may have been called that to her face *and* behind her back, Rahab didn't keep her "before" as her identity. Rather, Hebrews 11:31 makes her status clear: She became a woman of *faith*, effectively stepping into her "after." Although the Israelites gave her "a place outside the camp" after her rescue (Joshua 6:23, NIV), their resignation didn't stop God from bringing her inside His family tree.

While it's all too easy to identify ourselves based on our past or current circumstances, we, too, can follow Rahab's footsteps and claim the new life, new spirit, and new identity Christ gives. In Him, God already defines your identity as follows:

- a friend of Jesus (John 15:15)
- loved at all times (Romans 8:35-37)
- redeemed (Romans 3:22-25)
- protected and upheld (Psalm 3:3; 55:22)
- bold and confident (Psalm 138:3)
- His work of art (Ephesians 2:10)
- a fearless powerhouse (2 Timothy 1:7)
- strong (Psalm 28:7)
- more than a conqueror (Romans 8:37)
- FREE (2 Corinthians 3:17)

It's up to you. Will you fall back on the labels that culture, your past, or mere people slap on you? Or like Rahab, will you believe who God says you are and watch how that new identity unfolds and comes to fruition?

TAKE THE NEXT STEP

How do you need to let Christ redefine you and your identity today?

PREPARE FOR WHAT *He's preparing*

1. Armor up—not for victory but from it
2. Don't settle for less than God's best
3. Help others seize their God-given territory
4. Be selective in entrusting certain details to godly men + women
5. Fear God over our fears
6. Attack old lies giving the enemy a foothold

7. Wait with purpose, knowing God is on the move
8. Believe it to see it
9. Find salvation under the blood of Jesus
10. Live in your before-and-after story

MILEPOST 3

Let's Move Out

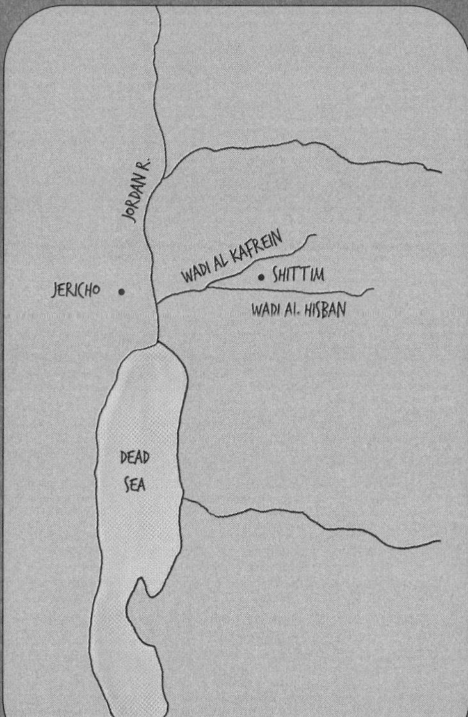

Are you observant?

I can take a sip out of my husband's water, leaving no trace of evidence, and he still knows. (Then refuses to drink anymore, because apparently, that's gross . . . **yet has no problems exchanging saliva at other times, if you catch my drift?**)

Maybe that was too far . . .

Anyways, these next ten days, there will be events that would've been visible to the naked eye (**now only PG-rated**)—but there will also be things unseen that matter above all else.

You'll see the floodwaters at the Jordan River, but don't miss what's also happening upstream in the city of Adam.

You'll come face-to-face with the miracle of the river's parting, but don't overlook the reason God privately gives to Joshua.

You'll notice the Ark of the Covenant, but don't lose sight of its exact positioning.

You'll learn the date of events, but don't look past the anniversary.

And you'll come face-to-face with circumcision (**uff da, PG-13?**), but don't let the heart of the matter escape your notice.

All in all, God's reasons and ways are an undercurrent throughout every step of this journey—and catching a glimpse of that *then* is how we catch a glimpse of it *now*.

Lord, give us eyes to see . . .

21

But How?

Joshua 3:1-4

Ever know WHERE you want to go, but have no idea HOW to get there?

Wherever I fly for speaking engagements, coffee is top priority. I crowdsource and get solid recs from my Instafriends, so, sure, I know WHERE I want to go . . . but I have zero clue HOW I'm gonna get there. What freeway to take? How far away is it? Can I speed, or do people abide by the law here? Because I've never been to these cities! It's all new to me.

This is how the Israelites felt. **I'll concede, they weren't looking for breves.** But they knew where they wanted to go: the Promised Land, their future home. But . . . *how?*

More than just cruising around in their rental, these Israelites were looking ahead at what was normally a narrow river. Yet now, in the springtime, it was flooding so much that it filled up this valley—almost 150 feet deep and a mile wide in places.[1]

To say they were in over their heads would be an understatement.

Where do *you* feel in over your head? You're standing on the banks of your marriage, looking across the flood of your kids' lives, or feeling the strong waves lap against your health.

You know where you want to be.

You want to love your spouse again.

You want that child that owns your heart to get back on the straight and narrow.

And you want to feel good again. You want your energy back. You want the doctor's appointments to cease and your freedom to return.

Like the Israelites, you know WHERE you wanna ultimately be, but it seems so far-off. The current feels bigger and stronger than what you have left in you. The absolute mess of the flood makes any crossing look impossible.

Good news: God positioned His people in this very spot—*on purpose*.

Not out of cruelty or as a means to dish out punishment. No, as our Helper who is forever faithful to His own, God specifically set them up and showed up through the Ark of the Covenant to lead the way. All they needed to do was keep following Him.

It really was that simple. With the Ark ahead, "you will know which way to go, since you have never been this way before" (Joshua 3:4, NIV).

Fast-forward to the New Testament, and time and time again, Jesus repeated this same directive: "Follow me" (in Matthew alone, see 4:19; 8:22; 9:9; 16:24; and 19:21).

The call has always been simple, but we tend to panic in the face of the unknown and doubt while looking on at the rising waters, making the situation more complicated than it was ever meant to be. Today though, let's respond differently, for . . .

He knows the way.

He will make a way.

He is the Way.

TAKE THE NEXT STEP

How do you need to follow today?

22

Consecrate Yo'selves

Joshua 3:5

Conse-**what?**

Listen, I grew up in the church, and while I admit I used to see that upbringing as **such boring material** for a testimony, I now see it as one of my favorite gifts from the Lord. As a mom, I realize, isn't that what we're all praying for? There's nothing better than our kids coming to know Jesus at an early age, and man, what a blessing to have the grace of God covering as much of our lives as possible, AMIRIGHT?

But between you and me, even after all these decades, I still get confused about ambiguous church lingo. Like *propitiation. Sanctification. Synoptic. Atonement. Canonical. Eschatology* . . . I mean, I'm not bilingual. I dropped out of Spanish in college, so where's a translator?

You seem like an intelligent person (**why else would you have bought this book?**), so maybe you speak Christianese and can recite the definitions of those words better than dictionary.com.

But if I was in this herd overhearing Joshua's simple proclamation, "Consecrate yourselves" (Joshua 3:5, NIV), my eyes would've darted every which way, shuffling to blindly follow my neighbor—who knows where ***(just with the hope that at the minimum, the journey included food)***.

Here's the deal: If you read *P.S. It's Gonna Be Good*, you know Google is a liar. And while that's true particularly in diagnosing illnesses, I'll concede the search engine is usually spot-on with its definitions. After a quick search, we'd find *consecrate* means "make or declare (something, typically a church) sacred; dedicate formally to a religious or divine purpose."[2]

We see this in a few different ways in Scripture. When God called for Israel's consecration at Sinai (Exodus 19:10-15), it looked like washing their clothes. Not unlike when Jacob's entire household was instructed to put away their foreign gods and change their clothes (Genesis 35:2).

As someone who's always listed shopping at the top of my favorite hobbies, I'd like to note both instances required a good wardrobe change. #icangetbehindthat

But in Joshua's case, we see the call was a spiritual purification "in turning the heart to God, in faith and trust in His promise, and in willing obedience to His commandments."[3]

(Although I'm sure a quick outfit change wouldn't hurt either?)

I digress.

The point: Wherever you are on the river's edge today, with nothing but the unknown ahead, the call to consecrate yourself still stands. God is indeed up to something and about to "do amazing things among you" (Joshua 3:5, NIV). In the meantime, we each have a personal responsibility before we enter a new land, a new season, a new level: to get right first, with God and others.

TAKE THE NEXT STEP

What does consecration look like for you? How do you need to turn your heart back to God? Where do you need to put aside stress, disappointment, and worry and move forward in faith? What commandment do you need to (willingly) obey? And who do you need to go to today to make things right?

Today is the day. "Tomorrow the LORD will do amazing things" (Joshua 3:5, NIV), most definitely, but today is for consecration . . . (and if you feel the need to also shop for a new outfit, I can see biblical grounds for that too).

23

It's Going Down for Real

Joshua 3:13-16

I don't like to walk into my kids' rooms without seeing where I'm going. **If you know, you know.** Their floors are nothing but a battleground—full of land mines disguised as tiny LEGO bricks and necklace beads I'm sure are fully determined to pierce my feet and scar me forevermore.

So if it's dark? I switch on my phone's flashlight.

If it's during the day, well TBH, I just steer clear until all is clean (**and safe**).

Here's the problem: We can't always do that in life. As much as we'd like to see the path cleared before moving forward in a new job, a new town, a new direction, we're limited human beings without the ability to see beyond our peripheral vision and into the future.

The Israelites were no different.

I'm sure it would've felt much safer and more reassuring to wait until the waters stopped rushing *before* wading into the Jordan. But the Lord specifically told the priests to set foot in the Jordan, and *then* "its waters flowing downstream will be cut off" (Joshua 3:13, NIV).

Look upstream, and you'd see nothing but a flood at its deepest stage. The opposite way? Everything in the river's path is being carried downstream. No sign of the beast stopping . . . **yet you're told to step right in.**

If you're facing the roar of life's waves, good news: There is more going on than you can see, and God is already moving pieces into place. You are safe to move forward.

In the Israelites' case, God was working in the city of Adam, in the vicinity of Zarethan, a great distance away (Joshua 3:16)—about twenty miles upstream from where they were standing.

This means Adam was totally out of sight for the Israelites. Even with binoculars and twenty-ten vision, they could not have witnessed what God was up to upstream, but it was *up there* that God "completely cut off" (Joshua 3:16, NIV) the water. I feel the need to repeat: God did not stop the waters directly in front of the Israelites. But miles away, He caused the Jordan to "pile up in a heap" (verse 16, MSG).

But they didn't see the domino effect until they stepped in.

In the same respect, Peter had to *climb out* of the boat to walk on water. Joshua had to *go in* to battle before he saw the sun stand still. And the servants had to *draw out* and *take* the water to the master of the banquet before they saw it turn into wine. We, too, have to walk out in faith before we'll see the hand of God move—by trusting that He's already got it worked out upstream.

TAKE THE NEXT STEP

What does that step into uncertainty look like for you?

Don't hang back, but be certain of what you don't see (Hebrews 11:1). May today be the day you take that plunge in faith, trusting God to be faithful in the unknown, already preparing the way.

24

Set Out, for It's Only a Setup

Joshua 3:7-16

How have you seen God use something in your life multiple ways?

Years ago, I sat at our kitchen table with my brother, both of us in the same college speech class at the time. We were talking about how fun it would be to be a speaker for a living, but then he made a good point: "Doesn't it feel like most messages and platforms are birthed out of some sort of tragedy?"

I laughed and waved off the idea: "Yeah, never mind—*I don't want that!*"

Then . . . I was diagnosed with cancer.

And now I'm a traveling speaker sharing my testimony.

> "Well, well, well, how the turn tables."
>
> THEOLOGIAN MICHAEL SCOTT

But here's what I love: God is so complex that no act has one single purpose.

In other words, yes, He parted the Jordan River so the Israelites "will know that the living God is among you and he will certainly drive out before you" all the rival nations (Joshua 3:10, NIV)—giving His people fuel for their faith for the day they would face their enemies.

But that wasn't His only purpose.

God spoke a private word about it directly to Joshua. Using His personal, intimate name, the Lord zeroed in on His faithful leader and declared, "Today I will begin to exalt you in the eyes of all Israel, so they may know that I am with you as I was with Moses" (Joshua 3:7, NIV).

God was blessing His people through this miraculous parting, no doubt, and it was indeed done to showcase His power, His care, and His faithful leading over all.

But it was also to set up our guy Joshua.

Moses was the only leader these people had known, so Joshua was bound to be met with hesitation, if not skepticism. Yet God had chosen him for the job, and here He orchestrated events in a way that would win His people over.

It was this flood stage, this impossibility, that would be Joshua's defining moment as a leader and set him up for success.

In the same way, I found God was using my cancer journey to draw others to Himself. I witnessed thousands praying for me. Some were opening up to conversations about Christ, when they were previously closed off. And every single observer had a front row seat when God cut my chemotherapy treatments in half.

The miracle was clearly to showcase God's sovereignty, goodness, and active work in our lives. But what I love is that it was done not just for all the witnesses, **but for me too**.

He gave me reassurance He was not done with me yet.

He gave me strong evidence that He still had a purpose for my life.

He gave me a story to share. A means to use my spiritual gift of teaching and encouragement. A dream come true to speak to the masses about the truth that set me free.

And He's doing something for you too. Since our God wastes nothing and wants to use every single thing that enters your life for your good *and* His glory (Romans 8:28), you'll get both. He may be doing something for other people, but He's doing something for you too—in an intimately personal way, packaged as a good gift tailor-made **just for you**.

TAKE THE NEXT STEP

How can you set out today knowing that whatever's ahead is purely a setup—for you *and* for bringing comfort to others (2 Corinthians 1:3-7)?

Flip your perspective on the obstacle ahead and rest in the fact that God is in control, has a plan, and has your best interests in mind too.

25

Pick Up Your Stone

Joshua 3:17–4:24

Has something tilted your world upside down, leaving you shaking your head and asking, "WHAT JUST HAPPENED?"

This was one of those moments for the Israelites. "The priests who carried the ark of the covenant of the Lord stopped in the middle of the Jordan and stood on dry ground, while all Israel passed by until the whole nation had completed the crossing on dry ground" (Joshua 3:17, NIV).

Isn't that just how life goes? For years, these people dreamed of the Promised Land. They spent days on the edge of the Jordan preparing to cross. We're given chapters of the pregame. Then, *snap* just like that, in the scope of one verse, these two-million-plus children of God cut across the dry ground like NBD and stepped into their long-sought homeland. It could've taken them about an hour if they marched in a square of about 1,000 people across and 2,000 people deep.[4]

Make no mistake: You may spend years preparing for your future career. You may daydream for days, reading up on all things motherhood before your baby actually comes. And you may exercise, tweak your diet, and test out different supplements for endless chapters of your life before you finally reach your fitness goal.

Most of life is this way: preparation. But when the diploma is handed to you, the baby decides to arrive, and you wake up one morning in good health, it can feel like your entire reality just shifted in the blink of an eye. As you look around, stunned at your new circumstances, you shake your head like, **What just happened?**

So don't give up hope: You, too, may be only one sunrise away from the breakthrough.

But when you do get there—before you leave the past in the past and run full steam into the dream ahead—be sure to pause as Joshua did. He commanded twelve men representing the twelve tribes of the Israelites to each pick up a stone and make a memorial, and there's work for us to do, too, before we move forward in the blessing. Make your own memorial today—something you and others can physically *see*—whether in the form of a photo book, journal, Instagram post, or bracelet.

What would be the purpose? I see three important reasons that still stand true today:

1. When future generations ask about your memorial, you have the opportunity to share what the Lord has done (Joshua 4:21-23).
2. "So all the nations of the earth might know that the LORD's hand is powerful, and . . ."
3. ". . . so you might fear the LORD your God forever" (verse 24).

People are watching, questions will come, and your own faith is at stake. Make that memorial, then ask God to give you the boldness to share when someone looks at it or asks about it. We can so easily forget, but there are some things that should never be forgotten.

TAKE THE NEXT STEP

What has the Lord done for you, and how can you make a memorial in remembrance of it?

Jesus said, "You will be my witnesses . . . to the ends of the earth" (Acts 1:8). What does a witness do? They give evidence and testify. It's as simple as that.

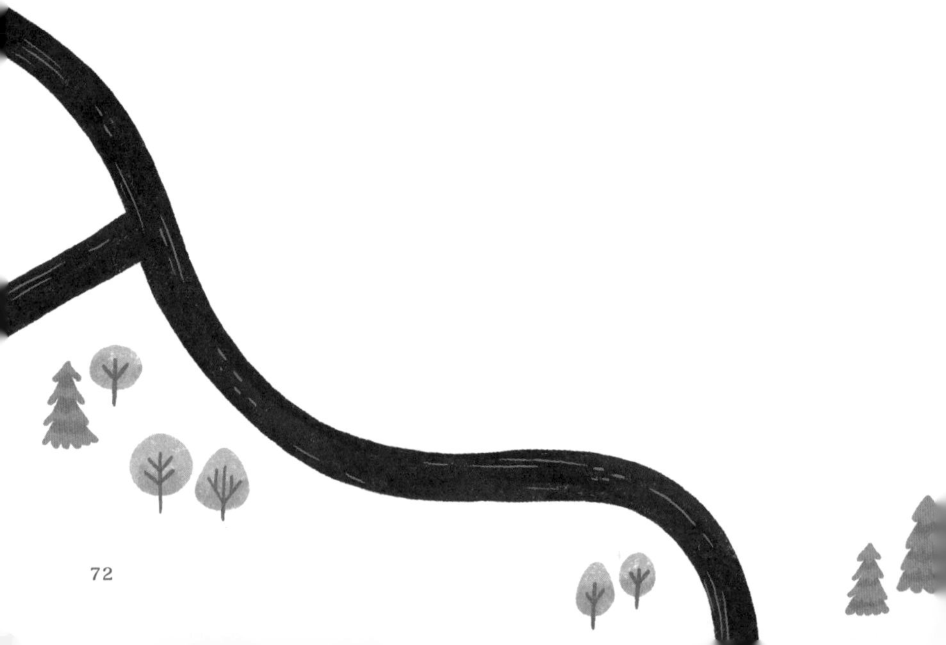

26

Hands Up—You're Surrounded

Joshua 3:17–4:24

Don't you hate being blindsided?

From the curveball of cancer to my husband simply rounding the corner without a sound, there are some surprises I could live without. In fact, considering how often I've been startled in my own house, I'd probably live longer, too, **you know, without the spikes in blood pressure.**

Maybe your husband is also an unaware stealth ninja.

Or those unexpected bills knocked you back.

Or a sudden injury, letdown at work, or call from left field shocked you.

We've all been there. Since we don't have eyes in the back of our heads nor a crystal ball to see into the future (since, you know, God's pretty against those—see: Leviticus 19:31), we will all at some point be sucker punched in the gut. **(Isn't this such an encouraging devotional?)**

But here's the good news: There is more than just you looking after you. God actually designated Himself your Helper and personal bodyguard. "The LORD will keep you from all harm—he will watch over your life; the LORD will watch over your coming and going both *now and forevermore*" (Psalm 121:7-8, NIV, italics added).

Since the Ark of the Covenant represented God's presence among His people, don't miss its position in the crossing of the Jordan River.

At first, it was carried in front of the people, where God divided the waters, making the way and leading the way.

Next, as the people followed, the Ark was stationed in the middle of the riverbed, as if guarding God's people at the halfway point, exuding His authority and strength over their circumstances, and standing in their midst along the journey. It stayed put "until all of the LORD's commands that Moses had given to Joshua were carried out" (Joshua 4:10).

Finally, once "everyone was safely on the other side, the priests crossed over with the Ark of the LORD as the people watched" (Joshua 4:11). The Ark went last, as if God had their backs too.

Do you see it? Psalm 139:5 says it best: "You hem me in behind and before, and you lay your hand upon me" (NIV). The New Living Translation puts it this way: "You go before me and follow me. You place your hand of blessing on my head."

This is your reality no matter if you're standing at the brink of the unknown, walking in the middle of the miracle, or looking back at what God has led you through: He goes before you. His presence surrounds you. And "the God of Israel will be your rear guard" (Isaiah 52:12, ESV), or in other words, He "will protect you from behind."

But your focus matters. You can look to the side and get caught up by the raging waters. You can look ahead and be consumed with fear over your enemies. And you can look behind and let the bitterness or disappointment of the past rule the day.

Or you can "keep [your] eyes always on the LORD. With him at [your] right hand, [you] will not be shaken" (Psalm 16:8, NIV).

TAKE THE NEXT STEP

Where is your focus today? How can you fix your eyes on the Lord instead?

When we keep the right perspective, we can breathe easy, knowing He's got us, and we're surrounded—in the very best of ways.

27

Passed Over on Passover

Joshua 4:19-24

Are you good with dates?

I had to sign a waiver for my kid to create bath bombs (**dangerous place, that Buff City Soap**). But first I needed to check the date with another mom who, too, was letting her kid do crazy things with essential oils. As I was about to say, "April 27?" she said, "May 4." Oh, okay . . . glad I asked.

So I'm gonna be real. When I first read Joshua 4:19, I skimmed right past that sucker: "The people crossed the Jordan on the tenth day of the first month." **Just semantics, right?**

Well . . . not so much. God had His people cross at this exact time for a significant correlation He didn't want them (**or us**) to miss.

Shall we dive right in?

This first month in the Hebrew calendar, aka Nisan, was the month God commanded the Jews to celebrate Passover. But even more eye-opening, it was on this very day (the tenth of Nisan), that Israel had been charged to select the animal for Passover (Exodus 12:2-3). Why? To commemorate their deliverance from Egypt.

Hold the phone. **(Do we still say that in the twenty-first century?)** When the calendar rolled around to Passover, the Israelites were observing their *own* passing over into the Promised Land.

Just as God delivered them from bondage decades ago, He was still seeing to their deliverance on this day.

And as they were celebrating and remembering all that God had done, exactly forty years after leaving Egypt (Deuteronomy 1:3), they were stepping into the very land God had promised since the beginning.

The Lord had saved them then, and He was still saving them now.

Did you need to know that too? We may trust that God saved us *before*, sure. He forgave us of our sins the moment we believed in Christ, yes. We will be saved on the day of judgment for all eternity, no doubt.

But . . . *now?*

When your business is failing?

When your relationships are strained?

When you're at the end of your rope in parenting?

When the current events of this world are driving you mad?

Who's to say He will save you *now*?

Make no mistake: The Lord is your Rock and your Fortress and your Deliverer (2 Samuel 22:2), and your Savior *still saves.*

No offense to the preceding generation of Israelites, but do you think they even *thought* to ask God to part the Red Sea? No. They assumed their only two options were to serve the Egyptians or die in the wilderness (Exodus 14:12).

In the same way, I don't know how God will deliver you and me—**I just know He will**. And when He does, the timing will be significant. He didn't usher His people into the Promised Land on the seventh month or even the twelfth. He teed it up in a way that these people would recognize the timing and could only attribute it to the faithfulness of their God.

Someday, the details will click for you too, and when the puzzle pieces fall into place and understanding dawns, surely the *why* will only leave you more convinced of your God's faithfulness.

TAKE THE NEXT STEP

How can you rest in God's timing today?

Let His faithfulness bring you peace in your current season of life.

28

Cut It Off

Joshua 5

What about God's timing do you not fully understand right now?

After four hundred years of slavery and another forty years of wandering in the wilderness, you can imagine these Israelites fresh out of the Jordan River, so eager to find a spot to call their own. **Pedal to the metal, full steam ahead!**

Between this momentum and then word spreading to the Amorite and Canaanite kings of their miracle crossing, leaving them "paralyzed with fear because of them" (Joshua 5:1), wouldn't it seem logical to strike out hard and fast while they had the advantage? *The time is now! If God is for us, no one can be against us!*

Yet even here, we see God's ways are not like ours.

Their green light flickers to yellow as God instead directs Joshua to pump the brakes, pull off on the side of the road, and circumcise this second generation of Israelites.

Hold up . . . *circumcise?!* Are we sure that's wise? I mean, this would immobilize the fighting men for *at least a week.* With the walls of Jericho just ahead, don't we need strength instead of weakness, confrontation instead of circumcision?

And dare we forget what happened with Simeon and Levi versus the

Shechemites back in Genesis 34? In revenge over their sister's rape, these brothers tricked the Shechemites into being circumcised—only to turn on them in their weakened state . . . *and kill them all.*

Will the fate of our men be the same? Like sitting ducks, an easy target for our enemies? And BTW, why *now*? Why didn't we do this *on the other side of the river*, when we were just chillin', safely out of reach of the enemy?

Things may not make sense in the moment, but later, we see how God set everything up. For one thing, the enemies were hiding behind walls, fearing their own demise. God knew this much—they could rest safely. For another, our Lord often uses outward things to symbolize something inward. Like "circumcise *your heart* and the hearts of your descendants, *to love the Lord your God with all your heart*" (Deuteronomy 30:6, NASB, italics added; see also Jeremiah 4:4). By this rite, these men were voluntarily and obediently taking off their old skin to figuratively step into the new. As a result, the Lord says, "Today I have rolled away the shame of your slavery in Egypt" (Joshua 5:9).

(He also named that spot the Hill of Foreskins, which is neither here nor there—just funny. **And now I fear my kids' humor is rubbing off on me.**)

But that's always God's MO. He wants to end *our* slavery as well. Cutting off our old, sinful nature so we can be made new. Healing what's ripped us apart, and taking away our shame to "[crown] you with love and compassion" (Psalm 103:4, NIV).

You must know, though, it will also involve us circumcising our hearts, cutting off the desires of the flesh, and letting the Spirit renew our thoughts and attitudes instead (Ephesians 4:23). Someday, you and I will understand His timing, but for now—we can trust Him to protect us as we obediently follow Him.

TAKE THE NEXT STEP

How can you join the Israelite men in obedience? How do you need to cut off the desires of the flesh and "let the Spirit renew your thoughts and attitudes" (Ephesians 4:23)?

You're safe to do so. He's given you space, so do the bloody, painful thing now, and then celebrate. You've "become a new person. The old life is gone; a new life has begun!" (2 Corinthians 5:17).

29

Different Bread, Same Bread of Life

Joshua 5:11-12

In my mind, I'm still twenty-eight. Do you, too, feel frozen in time somewhere? **(Or is this just a sign of a midlife crisis?)**

Hear me out: My traitorous driver's license *may say* I'm thirty-seven, but it feels like just yesterday, I was living in my college dorm. Just an hour ago, Ty and I got married. Didn't I pop out my first baby a mere *millisecond* ago?

But time will tell me no. I have been out of school almost as long as I was in it. A whole decade has passed since Ty and I exchanged our "I do's." And our oldest son has reached double digits.

Time is a thief, is it not?

But if time has taught me anything—it's that everything is only a season. Here on earth, nothing lasts forever. Even though we feel like this chronic illness, our marital strife, or the demands of our job are never ending, we are promised there is a beginning and end to every single activity under the sun (Ecclesiastes 3:1).

The Israelites had just hiked through the wilderness, and for that season, in the face of harsh conditions and scarcity of food, God took it upon Himself to shower His people with bread from heaven every day. Manna for breakfast, manna for lunch, manna for dinner. **Expected. Easy. *Miraculous.***

Yet now, upon entering a new season in the Promised Land, things were about to change. This was a new land. Different terrain. It would yield different crops and a harvest unlike any the Israelites could ever find in the wilderness.

So on this very day, when "they began to eat unleavened bread and roasted grain harvested from the land" (Joshua 5:11), God discontinued making His heavenly wafers drizzled with honey. "No manna appeared on [that] day . . . and it was never seen again" (verse 12).

No need to panic though. Just because the manna reached its expiration date, just because your paycheck stopped, just because that friendship ended does not mean God's provision has ceased too.

It's merely a change of seasons.

In the wilderness, He provided in a supernatural, miraculous way.

In Canaan, He provided in a natural way—planted, cultivated, and grown through His creation.

Both provisions came from God, and whether the season you're walking in is a time to plant or a time to uproot, a time to tear down or a time to build, a time to weep or a time to laugh, or a time to keep or a time to throw away . . . this same God who took care of the Israelites "will supply all your needs from his glorious riches" too (Ecclesiastes 3:2-8; Philippians 4:19).

TAKE THE NEXT STEP

How would you label the season you're in right now? Go through the list in Ecclesiastes 3:2-8 and circle the words that best describe it.

It's equally important to consider how God has provided for you in the past. While His provision may look different than it did yesterday, "Jesus Christ is the same yesterday and today and forever" (Hebrews 13:8, NIV). Jehovah-Jireh, our Provider-God, will continue to meet our needs.

30

It's Already a Done Deal

Joshua 5:13–6:2

Have you ever asked someone a question, but their reply in no way answered it?

My kids are the biggest offenders:

"Did you make your bed?" *"I found a frog."*
"Did you unload the dishwasher?" *"Look at my coloring sheet!"*
"Did you poop?" *"Mommy pooped."*

I'm still wondering. **(And my pants are clean, thank you very much.)**

Let's address something *a tad more important* than feces . . . Joshua bumped into an unfamiliar soldier standing right before him "with a drawn sword in his hand." As a man of war, Joshua had to know, "Are you for us or for our enemies?" (Joshua 5:13, NIV).

The Man replied, "No" (Joshua 5:14, ESV).

That doesn't help . . .

But He went on to say, "As commander of the army of the LORD I have now come" (Joshua 5:14, NIV).

Joshua immediately recognized this was no mere man, but *the* Son of Man. This was not just a military leader of an earthly realm, but *the* Leader of the *entire* host of heaven. **This was the one true God.**

Understanding the real chain of command, Joshua instinctively threw himself to the ground in reverence. "'I am at your command,' Joshua said. 'What do you want your servant to do?'" (Joshua 5:14).

As you look ahead at the obstacles blocking your own path and wait for God's direction, take note of Jesus' words.

He wasn't skirting Joshua's question to be difficult but to shed light on the right question. Not about *His* allegiance—"Are you for us or them?"—but about *ours*—"Are you for Him?"

Jesus doesn't follow *us*, bend to our demands, get in line to carry out our orders. He calls us to follow *Him*, and as much as our culture believes we can remain neutral, we all pick a side. Jesus Himself said, "Anyone who isn't with me opposes me, and anyone who isn't working with me is actually working against me" (Matthew 12:30).

Like Joshua, may we have the good sense to recognize who stands before us today, knocking at the door of our hearts, and fall down in awe-filled worship too.

As you echo his question, "What do you want me to do next, Lord?" be reassured this is exactly why Jesus came: to show how what appears to be impassable will certainly be made accessible through the power of God. The walls of Jericho were coming down—not by Joshua's strength, but *His.*

Like I say in *P.S. It's Gonna Be Good*, in Joshua 6:2, "God spoke about their deliverance in past tense for *a reason*. In His eyes, Jericho's defeat was as good as done."[5] The same is true for you. What may look like insurmountable odds, an unfought battle, or a brick wall is nothing to the One "who opens [what] no one can close" (Revelation 3:7).

TAKE THE NEXT STEP

In light of the challenges standing before you today, where is your focus: the walls of Jericho or the commander of the angel armies promising deliverance?

"You can believe in God's promises that haven't happened yet as if they already have—solely because He said they would."[6] In Christ, victory is *yours*, for that is exactly why He came.

HOW TO CROSS INTO the Land of Promise

1. Follow the Way for the way
2. Turn your heart to God + consecrate yourself
3. Step out in faith, certain of what you do not see
4. Set out in the challenge, knowing it's a setup for your good + His glory
5. Pick up a stone in remembrance

6. Focus on God's protective presence surrounding you today
7. Trust that the Lord who saved you is still saving you
8. Cut off the desires of the flesh + be free from shame
9. Bank on God to provide in each season
10. Focus on the Commander of Heaven's Armies vs. the walls ahead

MILEPOST 4

Normal vs. Unusual Battle Strategy

Ever been riding on a mountaintop high, only to be brought down low by some blow?

These next ten days, we'll watch the Israelites enjoy one of the biggest victories in the land, and tucking this incredible achievement under their belt, their confidence and morale will climb to an all-time high. Yet the very next battle?

. . . defeat.

What went wrong? And what gives when we face *our own* crushing losses?

Let me just say, instead of giving in to doubt, **you're gonna want to give God the benefit of the doubt**. Not only will you see what underscored their breakdown, but you'll regain some hope in the middle of yours too.

Ultimately, instead of letting yesterday's failure keep us from today's success, we'll remember that our God brings purpose in everything, He's on our side, and He's up to something new. Someday, when we see it for ourselves, we, too, will marvel at His strategy.

31

Gotta ~~Work for It~~ Rest in Him

Joshua 6:1-5

We live in a self-made, DIY world that repeats the same mantras:

Have a dream? *Make it happen.*
Didn't get it? *Just work harder.*
Want something done right? *Do it yourself.*

On the one hand, sure, if we want a dream house, a job will pay for it. If we want to grow a garden, gotta plant seeds. If we hope to get in shape, pounding chips on the couch (sadly) won't do the trick . . . this is my story, this is my song.

But like the serpent who twists truth so that it no longer *is* the truth, hustle culture's twisted the work of our hands to be something God never intended. It is no longer simply a means to get something done or a call to carry out, so we're running ourselves into the ground as if the entire weight of our success, livelihood, dreams, and destiny rests on our output. Like, you betta rise and grind because it's all on *you* to make the life you want.

But once again, God's thoughts are not like ours, neither are our ways His ways (Isaiah 55:8).

Case in point: Jericho was built on top of a tall hill and surrounded by double walls that "created the illusion of a fortified city nearly 10 stories in height from ground level."[1] The normal tactic for taking such a well-protected city was a siege. As in, wait it out . . . *for months* . . . until food and water ran out and desperation led to surrender.

But this wasn't the strategy God laid out for His people. Their marching orders were to take a power walk around the block once a day while the priests provided jazzy background music. After six days of reps and after circling seven times on the seventh day, it was time to join the Isley Brothers, kick up your heels and SHOUT, and witness the walls collapse.

Here's what's significant: The priests' horns weren't some rusty instruments left over from middle school band. These were the well-known shofars that were blown every Friday evening to mark the beginning of Sabbath.[2]

See what I'm seeing? God wasn't placing the weight of the battle on the Israelites' shoulders. All He wanted them to do was rest in Him. Depend on their God. Lean into His power and wait for His salvation.

I believe God is sounding the shofar for us too. When you're up against something far greater than you, when the obstacles are insurmountable and the victory feels impossible, you don't have to panic as if it all falls on you.

Like God rested on the seventh day of Creation, He wanted the Israelites to rest in Him on the seventh walk around Jericho. He invites us to do the same in the seventh hour of our own lives. Will we?

TAKE THE NEXT STEP

How can you follow suit and rest in God today?

Expect the unexpected instead of feeling constrained by the norm—"for just as the heavens are higher than the earth, so [His] ways are higher than your ways" (Isaiah 55:9).

32

Is It Insider Intel?

Joshua 6:6-14

Ever admitted a dream, goal, or plan to someone . . . only to have them respond skeptically and voice doubt?

Take this book for example. I know myself. If I saw even a hint of a furrowed brow or a cocked head in response to this travel-through-the–Promised Land idea, the uncertainty might have rubbed off on me. So I kept the concept hush-hush, processing it with only a few, until I knew deep down this was the direction God would have me take.

Our man Joshua is at a similar crossroads. He hears the battle plans from the Lord Himself, and in the very next verse, we see obedience. Without hesitation and with full conviction, he struts right over to the priests, calls together his army, and lays out the plan.

Except . . . wait. As we overhear Joshua relaying the to-do list, he misses something *noticeable*.

- ☑ Priests: Take up the Ark of the Covenant and jam on the horn.
- ☑ Warriors: March around the city.
- ☑ People: Stay silent until the conductor raises the baton.
- ☐ On the seventh day, march seven times, and when we raise a ruckus, the walls will crumble.

Do you see it? He told them what they needed to know *today*, but they weren't privy to what would come *tomorrow*. Parroting my kids' favorite question . . . but *why?* Why omit the most motivating part?

Well, let's remember who we're talking about here. Joshua had learned the hard way that not everyone can be trusted with all the details. Like their ancestors, if there's a chance these people would waver in faith and influence *others* to waver in faith . . . Nah. **Hard pass.**

Having been raised in the wilderness because of the older generation's skepticism, Joshua understood better than most the importance of believing God's promises over others' approval or uncertainty.

Not wanting to hang tight in no-man's-land any longer, Joshua used discernment on when and what to disclose and didn't open the door *an inch* to distrust.

When God lays out a path for us too, not everyone needs to know all the juicy details. Some things can stay between you and God, **and that's okay.** Like Joshua, you can be wise about who you confide in, and where He gives the green light, GO. The outcome is in God's hands, but obedience is always in ours.

TAKE THE NEXT STEP

Where have you been given the GO signal?

Consider what may be best to keep between you and God, and what it would be wise to share with others. Then take that next step of obedience today.

33

Hopelessly Devoted to You

Joshua 6:15-21

You know when you hear a word and instantly associate it with something from your past?

Like if you talk about the rapture, I'm immediately wetting my pants, picturing the *Left Behind* series.

If you ask, "Should I keep the candle burning?" I'll sing Point of Grace.

And if anyone says, "I'm diving in," you betta believe I'll finish, "I'm going deep, in over my head I wanna be."[3]

Another one of those words for me, although very much less Christian, is *devoted*. The lights dim, I'm standing beside Olivia Newton-John in matching white nightgowns, and we're belting out in harmony, "Hopelessly devoted to you."

Have I completely lost you?

Hang with me. The definition of *devoted* is to be "zealous or ardent in attachment, loyalty, or affection."[4] It's equivalent to being dedicated and committed exclusively to something or someone.

I've only ever pictured it as a positive thing, like the "electrifying" love between Sandy and Danny that defied all odds.

But following the Israelites around Jericho that seventh day, I hear it used in a completely different way. Joshua commands, "Shout! For the

Lord has given you the city! The city and all that is in it are to be *devoted* to the Lord" (Joshua 6:16-17, niv, italics added).

Yet not devoted in love . . . **but to destruction**. Very much for the negative.

This means even our enemy is "devoted" to the Lord. That impenetrable wall, the opposing force, that insurmountable challenge we face may seem rogue, out of control, and dictated by evil—yet, like Jericho, it must fall under His control. It must get in line to the sovereignty of His command, and it must bow in submission to His good plans that can never be thwarted.

The weapons formed against you face the same destiny.

Every disappointing, scary, or painful flaming arrow is bound to fizzle. This outcome is guaranteed and inevitable. Its predestined course is inescapable. Just as the walls of Jericho fell flat, so will the walls hindering His plans for you—because it all belongs to Him.

"The earth is the Lord's, and everything in it, the world, and all who live in it" (Psalm 24:1, niv).

But above all, don't forget: This God who holds authority over all, and to whom everything on earth is devoted, is fully devoted to *you*. In the purest, most positive definition of *devoted*, He delights in *you*. The cross is indisputable evidence that He loves you.

Will you reciprocate his devotion, or, like in *Grease*, will this be a case of unrequited love?

TAKE THE NEXT STEP

How can you dedicate your obstacles and challenges as hopelessly devoted to the Lord?

Dedicate those challenges to God today, and in turn, rest in His devotion to you.

34

Help Is on the Way

Joshua 6:22-25

Where's the hope when the walls crumble around you?

I feel ya. I remember going to the hospital for a biopsy and praying fervently for a miracle. You've heard the stories, too, right? People supernaturally healed. Could I be one of them? Like the woman in Mark 5, could I reach out to Jesus and instantly feel His power run through me? Hear Him say, "Daughter, your faith has healed you. Go in peace and be freed from your suffering" (verse 34, NIV)?

I wanted so badly for that to be my story. How awesome if surgeons, doctors, and radiologists were all dumbstruck over the results! I pictured them with jaws dropped to the floor, shaking their heads like, "How? No tumor? No cancer? It's a miracle!"

But my oncologist later confirmed a different reality. I did indeed have stage 2 cancer, and I'd need to go through six months of chemo and six weeks of radiation.

And so, the battle began.

But here's what I've found: While God may allow and lead us into certain battles, that in no way means He's forfeited the victory. Quite the opposite: Jesus has already overcome, and in Christ, God calls *us* overcomers too (Romans 8:37)—no matter what wars wage around us.

Rahab stands as a testament. We know girlfriend placed herself under God's protection, but notice, Rahab's saving didn't come before the battle.

God didn't usher her out of the city walls when the spies escaped nor before the final march. He didn't spare her from the battle scene.

But under His refuge, she waited. And what did she live to see? Psalm 91 in action:

> A thousand may fall at your side,
> ten thousand at your right hand,
> but it will not come near you.
> You will only observe with your eyes
> and see the punishment of the wicked.
>
> If you say, "The Lord is my refuge,"
> and you make the Most High your dwelling,
> no harm will overtake you,
> no disaster will come near your tent.
>
> "Because [she] loves me," says the Lord, "I will rescue [her];
> I will protect [her], for [she] acknowledges my name."
>
> PSALM 91:7-10, 14, NIV

When warfare surrounds you, even though you prayed for God's saving well before things got this far, follow Rahab's footsteps. Dwell in the shelter of the Most High and find refuge under the cover of His feathers (Psalm 91:4). Just as He did for this beloved woman and her family, God will show you His salvation and faithfulness.

When you acknowledge His Name, help is on the way.

TAKE THE NEXT STEP

What could it look like to wait like Rahab while the battle rages right outside your front door?

35

Give In to Doubt or Give God the Benefit of the Doubt

Joshua 7:1-9

Ever felt like God gave you the go-ahead—to get that new business venture off the ground, start trying for a family, or pursue that dream—but you had to slam on your brakes, due to a road closure? **What gives?**

During my battle against cancer, I created a blog called *Dear Mr. Hodgkin's*. After I realized it was being read and shared by thousands, I wondered, *Maybe not everyone likes to write? Maybe this is actually a gift?*

Which is why, after I reached remission and wrote a farewell letter to Mr. Hodgkin's, I tried launching a new blog, thinking, *Surely, if the Lord has blessed my hand to write, it'll succeed.*

It failed.

Few read it. No shares. No reward. After months and months of trying, the discouragement was too much, and I quit.

A few years later though, I still had the itch to write. With no outlet besides my own diaries, I created an Instagram account and started fresh.

Fast-forward, and that account now reaches a community of hundreds of thousands of women. It's also what introduced me to my publisher and led the way to my first book and then to this one.

The call to write was right. But the timing wasn't. It was just a red light at that intersection that would later turn green.

As Joshua's riding on a mountaintop high from the triumph over Jericho, we read, "The LORD was with Joshua, and his fame spread throughout the land" (Joshua 6:27, NIV). With this first victory under his belt, our boy is pumped and READY to seize it all. Onward, we go!

After he sends men to spy out the next town of Ai, the momentum was contagious. Grinning like foxes in a henhouse, they report, "No need for all of us to go up there . . . since there are so few of them," (Joshua 7:3). Joshua pumps his fist and dispatches 3,000 warriors, already tallying another W in the win column.

But then, "they were soundly defeated. The men of Ai chased the Israelites . . . and they killed about thirty-six who were retreating down the slope. The Israelites were paralyzed with fear at this turn of events, and their courage melted away" (Joshua 7:4-5).

Wait, what? They conquered Jericho, but they're driven from this small town? What are we missing? Why the setback?

When we, too, experience a loss when expecting a win, let's follow the way of Joshua. He went straight to God in prayer with his questions: "Why? And now what?"

When you face setbacks and see regression instead of progression, you have this same choice. You can either give in to doubt or give God the benefit of the doubt. As Joshua's story unfolds, we see this truth: You'll always regret the first option, but never the latter. Trust Him today.

TAKE THE NEXT STEP

What would it look like to give Him the benefit of the doubt in your own circumstances?

36

Sitting in the Question Mark

Joshua 7:1-9

When we read the Bible, it's all too easy to fast-forward to those highlight reels we all know and love.

Take Elijah. One man against 850 false prophets, instigating a God contest and calling down fire from heaven. No doubt, one of the best stories out there. Or Shadrach, Meshach, and Abednego thrown into a fiery furnace, but then Jesus Himself shows up; all four walk around unbound and unharmed! More suspense, high stakes, and drama than even Disney could dream up, IMO.

But when we skirt past their backstories and zoom in straight to the ending, we miss something important. Before the happy ending, those trials, giants, and hiccups *abounded*, resulting in that same stress, overwhelm, fear, and incompetence we feel. Yet God was never done in the middle. He was still on the move and faithful to the end.

By rewinding, we realize the only conclusion that makes sense whenever we face challenges is God must not be done and we must only be in the middle of our story.

Joshua understood this. He knew God intimately and His character personally, so looking back and forth between the promise and the defeat, something didn't add up. Instead of being concerned about what this meant for *himself* though, he showed he was a man after God's own heart when he asked, "What will happen *to the honor of your great name*?" (Joshua 7:9, italics added).

Let's be honest: Would we care about such a thing?

When defeat comes, do we grieve because of our own crushed dreams or what it may mean for the Lord's reputation? Are we most concerned about what we wanted or how nonbelievers will interpret God's character?

In the land in between, when victory is snatched out of our hands and we're confused about why God allowed that to happen, the question still stands: Are we most concerned about building *our* kingdom or *His*?

Uff da, talk about a punch in the gut. But here in the middle of Joshua's story, with way more questions than answers, let's follow his footsteps, bowing down to God in the middle of our own stories too. Someday, we'll see the reasons for any defeat, but today, let's reorient our hearts to their rightful rhythm. In chorus with Joshua, let's be concerned about bringing honor to our God's great name above all else.

TAKE THE NEXT STEP

How could you feel more concerned about honoring God's great name?

Honor is defined as regarding someone with admiration or treating someone with great respect. (It's also defined as saluting with a bow in square dancing,[5] but I think it's safe to say that wasn't the original intent?) Whatever comes to mind, let's do it. We'll never regret it.

37

I Came, I Saw, I Coveted

Joshua 7:10-26

Give it to me straight: Do you believe God is withholding something good from you? We aren't the first to wonder.

When Joshua seeks the Lord about this very question, God lays it all out. "Israel has sinned and broken my covenant! They have stolen some of the things that I commanded must be set apart for me. And they have . . . lied about it and hidden the things among their own belongings. That is why the Israelites are running from their enemies in defeat. For now Israel itself has been set apart for destruction" (Joshua 7:11-12).

So wait. Their defeat at Ai wasn't because God didn't hold up *His* end of the bargain? But because someone else didn't hold up *theirs*? **Bingo.**

Fast-forward to the next morning, and after a process of elimination, there's a last man standing: Achan. **(Fun fact: His name means trouble, which is exactly what he was.)**

Achan admits, "I saw . . . I coveted . . . I took . . . I concealed." This man's single-handed discontentment and deceit "corrupted the entire assembly of God's people and was directly responsible for Israel's military defeat and the deaths of thirty-six soldiers."[6]

I'd love nothing more than to slink away from this family drama, but even in the uncomfortable, don't miss this: "Sin is like a little yeast that spreads through the whole batch of dough" (1 Corinthians 5:6). As much as we'd prefer it didn't, our sin affects us all like a tumbling row of dominos.

I wish I could go back though, and shake Achan's shoulders to get him to see God was holding nothing back. He was ready to give him *the entire Promised Land*. There was plenty of food ahead. Beautiful land to farm. God would even have allowed him to take spoils from future cities. Achan would've been more than well-off.

But this first plunder, the silver, gold, bronze, and iron from Jericho, was to be set aside for the Lord. By giving God the firstfruits, His people were honoring Him with the best.

But Achan wanted that for himself.

Here's the deal: When we tithe, giving God at least 10 percent back from what He's so graciously given us, not only are we free to do *whatever we'd like* with the remaining amount, but *man*, does He multiply that 90 percent far more than we ever could with the full 100.

At this juncture, we see coveting has no place in the Promised Land with a God who doesn't withhold any good thing but provides for all our needs according to His glorious riches (Psalm 84:11; Philippians 4:19). **Really, truly, we can trust Him to give us more than we could ever ask or imagine.**

TAKE THE NEXT STEP

What would it look like to honor God with the firstfruits in your life?

If you haven't yet "honor[ed] the Lord with . . . the best part of everything you produce" (Proverbs 3:9), learn from Achan and let today be the day. (Then GET READY.) God will open the windows of heaven and pour out a blessing so great, you won't have room to take it in (Malachi 3:10).

38

Yesterday's Defeat Can Be Today's Victory

Joshua 8:1-17

Sometimes, I give up too easily. Can you relate?

Like if I can't untangle a necklace after five seconds, I've been known to bring it to my mom.

If I can't get a stain out of our clothes after the first wash, I bring it to my mom.

And if it takes too long to connect puzzle pieces—as in minute-to-win-it—I save it for my mom.

I'm noticing a common theme here . . .

But clearly, giving up and impatience often go hand in hand—and we definitely have the option of giving up before the entire puzzle of life comes together.

In the Israelites' case, they could've given up after that battle at Ai. I mean, their brothers were killed there. The Amorites proved to be competent warriors. And after this sound defeat, "the Israelites were paralyzed with fear . . . and their courage melted away" (Joshua 7:5).

I don't know where you also have a little anxiety over the past. You faced that really distressing circumstance. You clearly remember your own bad turn of events. To some degree, it chipped away at your courage. God knows how a past disappointment can rear its ugly head and keep us from stepping out again—for fear of failure.

After the covenant was restored and things were right between the Lord and the Israelites once again, God reminded Joshua, "Do not be afraid or discouraged. Take all your fighting men and attack Ai, for I have given you the king of Ai, his people, his town, and his land" (Joshua 8:1).

If *we* are hesitant to step back into a battle we've previously lost, here's what we need to see and remember: Just because it ended in failure before doesn't mean it won't end in success this time. God's denials yesterday may just be His delay for victory today.

Providing a different strategy this time, God led Joshua to send out thirty thousand of his best warriors instead of only the mere three thousand who had gone before . . . and this new plan of attack changed everything.

Know for certain today: Our God is the God of second chances. You may have faced loss previously, but "because of the loving devotion of the Lord we are not consumed, for His mercies never fail. They are new every morning; great is Your faithfulness" (Lamentations 3:22-23, BSB). Take Him up on that new slate today and rely on His new strategy to see you through. He still has more to give, and you have more battles to win.

TAKE THE NEXT STEP

What defeat from yesterday threatens to paralyze and stop you in your tracks today?

Consider how God's words to Joshua might reassure and enable you for a fresh attempt. Do not be afraid, for the Lord is with you.

39

How Fiery Darts Will Backfire

Joshua 8:18-26

You know what statistic has literally changed my life?

On any given day, we can think upwards of sixty thousand thoughts. But get this: 95 percent of them are the same ones from yesterday.[7] That means we just keep thinking the same stuff over and over and over again . . .

Which is great if those thoughts are all true. All encouraging, lovely, praiseworthy.

But with the father of lies on the loose, out to steal our hope, kill our peace, and destroy our faith, we shouldn't be surprised that 80 percent of those repeating thoughts are *negative*.[8]

That's why I started my podcast, *Trade a Lie for a Truth*. I not only realized how truly those stats reflected my own experience, but I also recognized that the enemy of my soul wasn't being that creative in his attacks. He kept aiming the same fiery darts at the same target, in the same way, repeatedly, consistently, persistently.

Like **what's that bump?** Turns out it was a tendon.

Wait, I feel something on the back of my neck. Pimple. Should probably shower more.

Stomach pain, colon cancer, am I dying? Oh, just IBS (which lemme tell you . . . feels like death, but apparently *is not* death).

All in all, I seem to have unknown symptoms that pop up far more than the average Jo. My guess is you, too, have felt attacked in a way that seems beyond coincidence. As if someone knows right where it hurts.

Just as the enemy of our souls is stuck in his ways, the enemy of the Israelites "[came] out to fight as they did before" (Joshua 8:5). Yet this time, the Israelites hightailed it in a big show, as if they had been scared off. Their hope was for the Amorites to puff out their chests in pride and assume, "The Israelites are running away from us as they did before" (verse 6).

And that's exactly what they did, playing right into Joshua's hands.

God then gave His people a new strategy that would turn the enemy's attack against themselves. In fact, this is the first time in Scripture that we find the word *ambush*, or the idea of lying in wait for someone.[9]

While it appeared the entire army of Israel was marching away from the town, five thousand men were secretly lying in wait west of Ai. Once all fighting men had been lured out, Joshua lifted his spear, signaling the hidden unit, who then entered the unguarded city, "quickly captured it and set it on fire. When the men of Ai looked behind them, smoke from the town was filling the sky, and they had nowhere to go" (Joshua 8:19-20). With the Amorite army sandwiched between the two troops, Israel. Was. Victorious.

When the enemy's attacks *on you* are getting old, remember that God is doing something new there too. Make no mistake: The Lord lifts His own hand over your life. Any bad thing intended against you, He will indeed flip for good (Genesis 50:20), leaving the enemy dumbstruck and defeated. **Victory is on its way.**

TAKE THE NEXT STEP

How have you witnessed the enemy's repeated strategy against you?

Find hope in the truths of the Israelites' story. Remind yourself: He is doing a new thing.

40

Round and Round We Go

Joshua 8:27-29

I'm at the point in my parenting journey where I'm still trying to convince my kids I'm fun. Ever been there?

Like sure, I might say no to watching that R-rated movie. I may not let you sleep over at a stranger's home. And I will probably say, "No snacks before bed!" (Even though, let's be real—as soon as the kids are tucked in nice and tight, *I'm coming STRAIGHT DOWN* for that midnight snack).

But I say no—not because I'm lame or a buzzkill (unless it's past 9:00 pm). No, I assure you, I am very much fun (**as I'm sure you are since you're reading this book**). I'm just giving a thumbs-down because I know something my kids don't, and whether or not they believe it, I actually do have their best interests in mind.

On the flip side, as an older daughter, I now understand a whole lot more of my parents' own choices than I did when I was young. Like if I had heeded my parents' warning and avoided staying up with my friends to watch Stephen King's *It*, I wouldn't have feared clowns from hell hiding in my shower drain for months on end.

Who would've thought?

Oh yeah, my parents . . . who knew better.

But no matter how much we grow up, it seems we still fall into this same cycle of disbelief. The Israelites were no different:

Obedience followed by victory.
Victory followed by blessing.
Blessing followed by pride and disobedience.
Disobedience followed by defeat.
Defeat followed by judgment.
Judgment followed by repentance.
Repentance followed by obedience.[10]

. . . the cycle continuing, round and round we go.

Between the first and second battles of Ai, we see one obvious difference. With the first battle, there were spies, detailed reports, and a confident reliance on themselves. But not once is it recorded that Joshua or any warrior turned to the Lord in prayer, asking for His help and guidance, or relying on His power. We hear no mention of God. Thus, pride.

But flip the page to the second round, and **it's all on God**. He comes up with the strategy. He's the One leading the charge. Even in the heat of the battle, Joshua is getting moment-by-moment advice from God, and he and his men are relying on God to save the day. These men are at the "obedience followed by victory" point in this cycle, and blessing is coming for them. These Israelites will get to keep the plunder and livestock that Achan coveted.

But what about us?

God always makes a way to obedience, and when we follow that pathway, victory is ours through Christ (Romans 8:37). Take the step of faithfulness, and know "God is able to bless you abundantly, so that in all things at all times, having all that you need, you will abound in every good work" (2 Corinthians 9:8, NIV).

TAKE THE NEXT STEP

Where do you find yourself today on the cycle, and how can you end where the Israelites did—in obedience?

Knowing obedience always leads to victory, let's you and I make a pact to carefully choose our next step to be one of faithfulness.

ON THE MOUNTAINTOP HIGHS
+ in the valley lows . . .

1. Instead of working to rest, rest in His work
2. Use discernment on what's insider intel between you + God
3. Everything is devoted to God + He is devoted to you
4. Know help is on the way even when the walls crumble
5. Instead of giving in to doubt, give God the benefit of the doubt
6. Honor God's great name above all else
7. Give God the first + best— He'll multiply the rest
8. Don't let yesterday's failure keep you from today's success
9. God will flip the enemy's attack for your good
10. Obedience always results in victory

MILEPOST 5

Enemies Must Bow Down

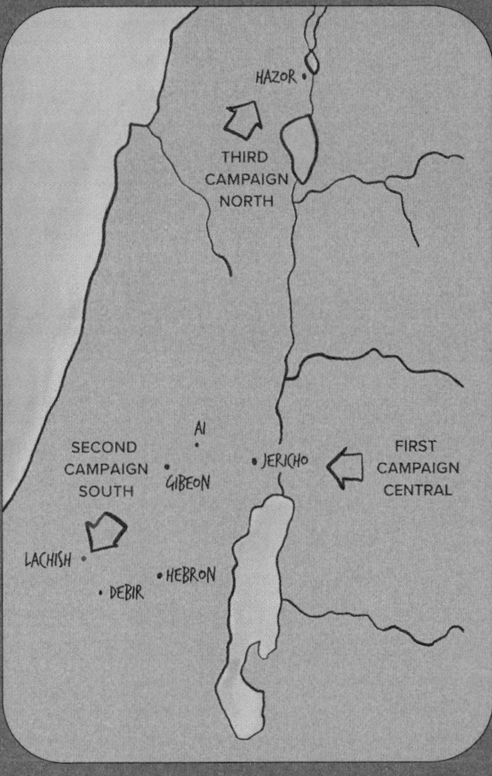

If the pessimists are right that we're either *in* a battle, *coming out* of a battle, or *heading into* battle, where do you find yourself today?

I hate to be a downer, but you'll find the Israelites enter each phase over these next ten days. Some of our battles are just as short-lived, but no matter how long they last, there's one truth we can't miss: The current fight doesn't put us or our future in jeopardy, **for the war is already won**. Sin, sickness, and death have already been overcome. If Christ is for us, nothing can be against us.

But all too often, we live our lives toying with the possibility that we could still lose. As if the fiery darts aimed at us hold the power to cause irreparable damage. As if the fight could lead to our demise. As if darkness could extinguish the light. As if our present weakness could destroy us.

Not anymore.

Like the Israelites, it's time to stomp on the neck of our opposition and see the trial for what it really is—merely an opportunity to seize and enlarge our God-given territory.

Get your game face on (**no makeup necessary**). It's time to move out and move in.

41

Will We Be the One out of Ten?

Joshua 8:30-35

Some people are very good at being present. Ty's like that. Are you too? Seize the day, enjoy the here and now, live in the moment. **#mustbenice**

Others—whether because nostalgia is sweet or there's regret or pain underneath the surface—they join Marty McFly time-traveling back to the past.

Then, there are those like me, who for better or worse often live in the future. We're the ones who stock our diaper bags and vans with everything under the sun **"just in case"** and have our five-, ten-, and fifty-year goals down *pat*. We're also the ones with active imaginations that (sometimes) get the better of us, projecting fears into the future that probably will never happen . . . **but we can never say never, you know?**

There are pros and cons with each knee-jerk reaction, but whatever ours are, we know all of the possible stumbling blocks for Joshua:

- He could've become a prisoner of the past, dwelling on all that went wrong, and become paralyzed by the possibility of it happening again.
- He could've gloated over his current success, turned complacent about how things were, and accepted this place as good enough.
- He could've taken advantage of their momentum, pushed toward victory in the next city, feeding into the desire for more, more, more.

Instead, he stops, builds an altar to the Lord, worships Him through offerings, and reads out loud to the Israelites "all the blessings and curses Moses had written in the Book of Instruction" (Joshua 8:34).

This isn't the only time we see gratitude as a virtue in God's book. In Luke 17:14, ten lepers begged Jesus for help. "He looked at them and said, 'Go show yourselves to the priests.' And as they went, they were cleansed of their leprosy."

Notice they weren't healed right then and there in the presence of Jesus. They had to walk away in faith and then find the officials to deem them healed and ready to be welcomed back into society. All of the lepers were made clean, but only one stopped in his tracks, turned around, and found Jesus to thank Him.

I can understand why the others skipped along—I, too, would be eager to reunite with my family, scoop up my kids in a big bear hug, and take an honest-to-goodness shower. But Jesus' response cuts me right to the heart: "Didn't I heal ten men? Where are the other nine?" (Luke 17:17).

Ever since I first read that, I've decided that I don't want Jesus wondering where I am.

Wherever you find yourself today, fight against living in the past or jumping ahead to the future. This is the day the Lord has made, and He wants you to rejoice and be glad in it (Psalm 118:24). But like the ten lepers, the choice is up to you. Before we bulldoze on to the next thing like the majority will do, let's follow the one leper and Joshua by thanking God, reading His commands that set us free, and worshiping Him today.

TAKE THE NEXT STEP

In the wake of a battle won and in light of God's many blessings, what do you need to thank Him for today?

Instead of just moving on to the next thing, choose not to leave Jesus wondering where you are.

42

How Your Fears Will Run in Fear

Joshua 9:1-13

Word travels fast, doesn't it?

I know this from firsthand experience living in small-town USA. But with Facebook community groups and apps like Nextdoor, news accelerates everywhere at the speed of light these days, **amiright?**

Take the latest top news story. Every time I refresh my feed, there's a new picture of a raccoon in someone's back seat with the caption, "Found a stray dog . . . anyone's?" Half our town is stressed, the other half is roaring with laughter. It's the weirdest prank, but welcome to Minnesota. We have to pass the winter somehow.

I digress.

Back in the Promised Land, even without news notifications at their fingertips, word spread quickly among Israel's enemies about Jericho's and Ai's demise. After "all the kings west of the Jordan River heard about what happened," they decided their only chance of survival was to join forces (Joshua 9:1). From the hill country to the western foothills and the coast, they "combined their armies to fight as one" in hopes that their new alliance would give the Israelites a run for their money (verse 2).

Well, all their armies . . . except one.

Meet the Gibeonites. Although their own town had its own mighty army, they believed the rumors and weren't so keen to go up against this God who squashed the powerhouses of their day. Maybe the others could buy some time, but these Gibeonites stood in close proximity to the Israelites. Realizing they could very well be the next target, they came up with a different plan.

Instead of donning armor, they "put on worn-out, patched sandals and ragged clothes" (Joshua 9:5). Packing dry, moldy bread along with old, patched wineskins and weathered luggage, they came posing like worn-out foreigners from a faraway land—when in actuality, they were neighbors posting photoshopped raccoons in their back seats.

Why the fanfare?

These Gibeonites had come face-to-face with the truth. Clearly, Israel's God, who defeated the world's superpower, Egypt, parted the Red Sea for His people to cross, and then dismantled the fortified walls of Jericho, could not be bested. No number of combined nations would be a match against Him, and the Gibeonites didn't want to be on the wrong side.

Do you realize this is the same God you serve today?

It may seem like evil is winning. Our twisted culture has the upper hand. And sickness and death still prevail.

But God is the same today as He was yesterday and will forever be. Just like Jesus gave "orders to impure spirits and they obey[ed] him" (Mark 1:27, NIV), by His Word, the demons still run and flee. With Him living inside you, you hold this same power. "I have given you authority to . . . overcome all the power of the enemy; nothing will harm you" (Luke 10:19, NIV).

Remember your reality today: "You, dear children, are from God and have overcome them, because the one who is in you is greater than the one who is in the world" (1 John 4:4, NIV). Your fears picked the wrong fight *for they're on the wrong side.*

TAKE THE NEXT STEP

Like the Canaanites banding together, how do you feel your troubles have teamed up against you? How is God calling you to take authority over the enemy?

God is still the One who makes your fears run in fear, so don't back down. Whatever you face today, lift your chin knowing all of heaven has your back.

43

The Key in the Question Marks

Joshua 9:14-15

Looks can be deceiving, can't they?

You order that designer knockoff that a certain influencer convinced you to buy—only to receive another dupe gone wrong.

You drool over that ad of a perfectly stacked burger—but instead are handed a sloppily mushed mess that looks nothing like what was pictured.

Your toddler puts on a facade of pure innocence as she claims, "Not poopy"—until she turns around and is very much proven guilty.

(I may or may not have experienced all of the above lately.)

This is where the Israelites stood. God had said in no uncertain terms, "Do not leave alive anything that breathes. Completely destroy them—the Hittites, Amorites, Canaanites, Perizzites, Hivites and Jebusites" (Deuteronomy 20:16-17, NIV).

Talk about a lot at stake. No wonder they were hesitant as they felt out the situation with the Gibeonites. "How do we know you don't live nearby? For if you do, we cannot make a treaty with you" (Joshua 9:7).

But these strangers must've taken a cue from my daughter as they convincingly professed, "This bread was hot from the ovens when we left our homes. But now, as you can see, it is dry and moldy. These wineskins were new when we filled them, but now they are old and split open. And our clothing and sandals are worn out from our very long journey" (Joshua 9:12-13).

As the Israelites took in the Gibeonites from head to toe, it all seemed true. *By the looks of it*, they were stating the facts. They indeed *appeared* to be foreigners. They *acted* like people from a faraway land.

But things aren't always as they seem, and the eye can be easily fooled.

As we stand before our own puzzles, unsure of the decision to make or the direction to take, praise the Lord we aren't left to our own devices. Instead, we need only lean in to the Israelites' experience to learn how to move forward in peace and confidence.

"The Israelites examined their food, but they did not consult the Lord. Then Joshua made a peace treaty with them and guaranteed their safety" (Joshua 9:14-15).

Just a mere chapter ago, our guys were living large in the "obedience followed by victory and blessing" part of the cycle. But just a flip of the page and already they've returned to defeat . . . ***How?***

Pride.

In the face of a question mark, these men felt no need to consult the Lord. They leaned on their own perception, relied on their own interpretation, depended on their own intellect, and banked on their own wisdom. But the call has always been to "trust in the Lord with all your heart and lean not on your own understanding; in all your ways submit to him, and he will make your paths straight" (Proverbs 3:5-6, NIV).

Good news: The way they tripped up doesn't have to be our slipup too. In direct contrast, how about our stories instead read, "After God's people examined the evidence, they consulted the Lord"?

TAKE THE NEXT STEP

Like the disguised Gibeonites, what circumstances are confusing you today?

God never asks you to figure it out on your own. His Word specifically states, "If any of you lacks wisdom, you should ask God . . . and it will be given to you" (James 1:5). Don't waste another moment—He's only waiting for you to ask. Then, you can wait in trust, for He *will* make your path straight.

44

Victors Not Victims

Joshua 9:16-21

How have you been wronged?

The cat just puked all over my white rug . . . moments after he snatched our family meal straight off the dinner table before I could catch him. (Yes, this has happened more than once.) So I'm not gonna lie: I had zero sympathy when I heard the regurgitating gags in the next room over. Serves him right, you know? He can't even enjoy his cheated meal? *Justice served.* The trickster had it coming.

But the laughing soon stopped when realization dawned . . . I (**read: Ty**) must clean it up.

Justice denied.

(Unrelated: How long do cats live again?)

We've all had someone pull a fast one on us, so it's easy to empathize with the Israelites when "three days after making the treaty, they learned that these people actually lived nearby!" (Joshua 9:16). Just as I'm more than ready to ship our cat off to my in-laws' farm, the people of Israel were ready to send these double-crossers packing too.

But Joshua shows us that how we respond after we've sinned and have been deceived is just as important as how we act prior to the decision.

While Joshua could've lashed out and put the Gibeonites to the sword, he didn't. Even amid the frustration and while looking at future implications, our guy stands by his word, realizing there is no alternative: "Since we have sworn an oath in the presence of the LORD . . . we cannot touch them" (Joshua 9:19).

It mattered to Joshua to be a man of truth, even if others spoke lies. Does it matter to us too? We can't control how people act, nor can we alter the future or diminish the ramifications of sin. But when the inevitable happens, do we stoop to our opponent's level, trade punch for punch, retaliate? Or will we follow Joshua's footsteps and reflect the character of our God who remains true to His Word?

God flips every bad thing for good, so we shouldn't be surprised at the outcome for Joshua. Although the Israelites deviated from obedience and allowed the enemy to infiltrate their camp, God delegated His authority to His people to exercise over the situation. By making the Gibeonites into woodcutters and water carriers specifically for the house of God, the Israelites made sure these tricksters were tasked to serve in a way that put them under the Israelites' authority and forced them to acknowledge the one true God in worship—*on the daily*.

God will do the same with the opposition in your life.

Even if adversity enters your camp, it must bow in submission to the greater Spirit dwelling within you. It must bend to serve God's good purposes for your life. Don't get that turned around. You are not dominated by evil, trials, or sin. No, the stark truth is you're a victor, not a victim. "Thanks be to God, who gives us the victory through our Lord Jesus Christ" (1 Corinthians 15:57, ESV).

TAKE THE NEXT STEP

What represents the Gibeonites in your life today?

God has given you the upper hand. Allow this truth to change your perspective and your position in the fight. You're a victor, not a victim!

45

Attacks Are Invitations to Advance

Joshua 10:1-8

Who or what makes you feel most vulnerable?

While writing this, I scheduled an appointment to have my doctor look at a suspicious lump. I was patting myself on the back for pushing back panic and remaining in peace as I waited it out, but that wasn't the only problem threatening to weigh me down. My husband was getting chewed out by a client on tough work calls. My son was the target of a ruthless punk with a pink bow. And my mom was dealing with a persistent cough that kept her home.

We know "the devil prowls around like a roaring lion looking for someone to devour" (1 Peter 5:8, NIV). **But I gotta tell you—there's another layer that's even more disturbing.**

When you make progress and overtake strongholds set against you, like I've done while waiting for medical appointments, this makes the enemy mad. If he can't get past your God-given armor, he doesn't simply give up though. He expands his search. By widening the radius, exploring further out, our adversary detects where else you may be vulnerable . . . shifting his bull's-eye from you to those you love most, in hopes of getting under your skin. If this takes down your allies too, well, ***it's only collateral damage.***

With the Gibeonites switching sides, King Adoni-zedek of Jerusalem sent a call to arms to his neighboring Amorite kings, urging them to "come and help me destroy Gibeon for they have made peace with Joshua and the people of Israel" (Joshua 10:4).

Notice: The target wasn't Israel. Their sights were set on their *ally*.

Joshua could've panicked at the threat of this mass opposition. He could've given in to bitterness and frustration that these unwanted Gibeonites were proving to be a further thorn in his side. He could've deployed a safe number of his army, hanging back with the majority to retain possession of their current land.

But no. Not only did "Joshua and his entire army, including his best warriors, [leave] Gilgal and set out for Gibeon" as soon as he received word of the attack (Joshua 10:7)—but the Lord reassured him along the way: "Do not be afraid of them for I have given you victory over them. Not a single one of them will be able to stand up to you" (verse 8).

Hear the Word of the Lord today: Do not be afraid of what threatens you. He has given you victory over it, and if He is for you, not *a single thing* can be against you. Like the Israelites interpreting this threat as merely a cue to press in and claim more of the land, let's view the enemy's attacks as invitations to expand our God-given victory as well.

As we'll see in the next Scripture reading, the Israelites approached the Amorite armies head-on, taking them by surprise. The attack intended to punish the traitorous Gibeon and stop Israel's advance was flipped to bless them and give the Israelites advantage. They conquered more territory, and their conquest was now a success.

I believe our trials can do the same for us. As God takes us from glory to glory, we don't have to give up or give in when the enemy attacks us and those we love most. Instead, know for certain: You're only attacked because *you're advancing*. **The battle is only confirmation that you're progressing.**

TAKE THE NEXT STEP

How can you view your trial today as merely progress and an invitation to gain more ground?

If the victory truly is already won, then no weapon formed against you could ever prosper. Press on, go all in, and claim the land that in Christ rightly belongs to you.

46

March On

Joshua 10:9-11

Have you ever felt completely spent and on the brink of burnout . . . yet instead of the hoped-for break or breather, you're only thrown back into the ring for yet another round? I wish I could say no.

I remember the weeks that followed Dottie's birth. **At a whopping ten pounds, eleven ounces, girlfriend did a number on my body.** It was hard enough to heal while also dealing with breastfeeding trouble, lack of sleep, and three other kids demanding my attention. But I kept having throbbing headaches too. I would stand up and need to clutch my pounding forehead before I could move. I'd look out the window and freeze in pain. I'd sit up, and everything would go black.

Apparently, postpartum spinal headaches are usually diagnosed while you're still in the hospital. But six weeks later? My doc had never heard of a case like it. So after eliminating terminal possibilities, and with no treatment protocol in place, she snuck me in the backdoor of the emergency room for an epidural blood patch. After weeks of struggle, I was already scared and beyond tired. Now, with a medical procedure to recover from as well, I wondered how I would survive this season. How could I fight yet another battle when I had nothing left in me?

But I kept hearing this same whisper: "Come to me, all you who are weary and burdened, and I will give you rest. Take my yoke upon you and learn from me, for I am gentle and humble in heart, and you will find rest for your souls" (Matthew 11:28-29, NIV). Day by day, moment by moment, I took Him up on the offer and unexplainably found rest.

The Israelites faced a similar state of exhaustion. When they received word of the Amorites' coming attack, they were encamped at Gilgal, *twenty-five miles away* from Gibeon, where the battle would take place.[1] So without any beauty sleep, "they traveled all night" (Joshua 10:9) with the march mostly "uphill, carrying their weapons and gear,"[2] ready to charge right into the fight. And no coffee stop? Uff da!

The genius that is ChatGPT calculates, "On average, a well-trained military unit marching on flat terrain at a moderate pace might cover around 3 to 4 miles per hour. Assuming a pace of 3.5 miles per hour, it would take approximately 7 hours to march 25 miles without any breaks."[3]

So at the bare minimum of a seven-hour trek, you gotta imagine these men would've been exhausted before the battle even began. But as God always does, He showed up and threw the Amorite armies "into a panic, and the Israelites slaughtered great numbers of them at Gibeon" (Joshua 10:10).

You may not have any strength left. Your energy may be zapped, and what's ahead may feel far bigger than anything you have in you. Good news: God says in 2 Corinthians 12:10 that you can delight and take pleasure *in this very spot* because when you are weak, then He is strong.

Like the Israelites, "those who trust in the LORD will find new strength. . . . They will run and not grow weary. They will walk and not faint" (Isaiah 40:31). You can march on, even through the night, for God's strength, victory, and rest will find you on the other side.

TAKE THE NEXT STEP

Where do you feel tired, and how can you go to Jesus for strength?

Exchange your burdens for His light load. March on and trust in His presence to carry you through . . . even without a cuppa cappuccino.

47

Possible or Impossible Prayers

Joshua 10:11-15

Where does it feel like you're running out of time?

As you're looking for Mr. Right, wanting to settle down, hoping to have kids, you're at odds with the ticking of your biological clock.

Or with your kids ready to fly the coop, you feel there's still *so much* you want to teach them while they're under your roof.

Or with that aging parent, approaching deadline, or looming exam, you've reached the eleventh hour and wish for more hours in the day.

It is no coincidence that you're standing before the battle with the Amorites today.

Even after Joshua and his army traveled all night from Gilgal and "defeated them completely at Gibeon" (Joshua 10:10, NIV), the battle wasn't over. The Israelites pursued their enemy to Beth-horon—which was five miles west of Gibeon. From there they continued, "killing them all along the way to Azekah and Makkedah" (verse 10)—which was *another fifteen miles* farther southwest.[4]

As if a twenty-five-mile overnight hike wasn't enough, these men booked it another twenty. **Almost two back-to-back marathons, y'all**. Talk about miraculous strength!

Then, pairing the supernatural with the natural, God joined in the fight by sending down "a terrible hailstorm from heaven . . . kill[ing] more of the enemy than the Israelites killed with the sword" (Joshua 10:11). Think of it: The Israelites were hot on the tail of the Amorites, yet the hail selectively fell only on the opposition. God's protective care covers us *no matter* the battle raging around us.

Yet daylight was nearly gone, and Joshua felt the time crunch. The leftover enemy troops were escaping into the foothills of the central mountain ridge, about to be covered by the darkness of night. Time was of the essence, and hoping to avoid hide-and-seek in pitch-black, Joshua boldly prayed in front of all the people of Israel, "Let the sun stand still over Gibeon, and the moon over the valley of Aijalon" (Joshua 10:12).

I gotta admit, even with an overactive imagination, this prayer request wouldn't have even *crossed my mind.* **I probably would've gone the more practical route like, "Oh, God, gimme the strength" or "You slay while I pray."**

But "Lord, let the sun stand still"? Unthinkable. Improbable. Most definitely impossible.

Yet what happened? "The sun stood still and the moon stayed in place until the nation of Israel had defeated its enemies" (Joshua 10:13).

Craig Groeschel says it best: "What you pray about reflects what you believe about God. . . . If all we are praying for is a good day, or for God to bless our food, then maybe we don't really understand who God is or what He can do."[5] Since He's still answering "sun stand still" prayers, what do you say we ask for the impossible?

TAKE THE NEXT STEP

What "sun stand still" prayer do you need to pray today?

Let's boldly call on the God who "is able to do immeasurably more than all we ask or imagine, according to his power that is at work within us" (Ephesians 3:20, NIV). Wherever it feels like time is running out, know that "when we're accomplishing God's purposes, God runs the time clock."[6]

48

Multifaceted Purposes in Play

Joshua 10:11-15

When one thing can check off two boxes, all the better, right?

Take the kids outside while you weed the garden or shovel the driveway? **Play and work, check!**

Invite your parents to a sports game? **Socializing and entertainment, check!**

Give your baby a family name that also has biblical meaning? **Honoring and significance, check!**

Because God is so complex, we could never consider Him or any of His ways to be one-dimensional, and there are always multifaceted purposes in play behind His every move. Unearthing them is the fun part, IMO. And this battle against the Amorites is no different.

God no doubt answered Joshua's prayer because He "delights in the prayers of the upright" (Proverbs 15:8) and He's unquestionably a Good Father who loves to "give good gifts to those who ask him" (Matthew 7:11).

But there's more! If we dig further beneath the surface and turn our attention to those Amorites, we find that the prominent deities they worshiped were none other than the sun and moon. As in, these enemies were trusting in the setting of the sun to hide their escape in darkness. They were waiting for the moon god to bring them salvation.[7]

Aha! By extending the light for a whole day and holding the sun and moon in place, God was showing everyone which god is the one true God—not just over these two elements, but over all. He wanted even these unbelievers to know who He is, in hopes they would turn from idolizing creation to worshiping their Creator.

That's still His heart today. He wants to work through your prayers because He cares for you, yes. But as a Father who wants His lost kids home, God will also use your prayers to reach anyone far from Him.

He is so good to do both.

But wanna uncover an even deeper layer? We read "there has never been a day like this one before or since, when the LORD answered such a prayer" (Joshua 10:14). While that's true, the *opposite* happened fourteen hundred years later when God brought on the night prematurely at the cross.[8] "It was now about noon, and darkness came over the whole land until three in the afternoon, for the sun stopped shining" (Luke 23:44-45, NIV).

This God, who controls the sun and the moon and everything else in all of creation, also tells of a day when a new heaven and a new earth will come. In that day, both the sun and moon will no longer be employed, "for the glory of God illuminates the city, and the Lamb is its light" (Revelation 21:23).

He truly has control over all and can pause, speed up, obliterate, and re-create altogether. So put your trust in Him. "Because he bends down to listen, . . . pray as long as [you] have breath!" (Psalm 116:2).

TAKE THE NEXT STEP

What feels out of your control today?

If God can stop the sun and moon, defeat death and the grave, and create a whole new heaven and earth, then He is certainly in control of *that thing* today. Someday, we will see He's had not only *one* purpose behind our battles . . . but two, three, and even more. He wastes nothing.

49

Run the Path to Promise

Joshua 10:16

I've found the definition of fun to be very subjective.

For me, really any type of activity that involves sitting sounds like a blast. Reading, writing, drinking coffee, napping, posting on social media—yeah, **I'm (literally) down**, sign me up.

Whereas for Ty, the marker of a good time seems to be a lot of sweating. Like hiking with snakes and mosquitos, digging in the dirt and gardening, and running. None of these would even make *the bottom* of my list. **(Hence my favorite tee that says, "My cardio is a coffee run.")**

But here's what I'm getting at: We've all heard our faith journey described as "the Christian walk." There are verses that tell us to "walk by faith, not by sight" and "walk in obedience to his commands" (2 Corinthians 5:7, NKJV; 2 John 1:6, NIV). But these instances of *walk* seem to be synonymous with the verb to *live*. Live by faith, live in obedience, live as unto the Lord.

Now clearly, I'm the type who prefers walking over running—so in turn, I would love my faith journey to resemble a nice, leisurely stroll versus a body-aching, leg-protesting, breath-wheezing marathon. But

Hebrews 12:1 focuses not on the verb, but the *noun* of the Christian life: "Let us run with perseverance *the race* marked out for us" (NIV, italics added). It's far from a walk around the park, but equivalent to a marathon in which you need perseverance and perspiration to endure.

We know this for ourselves, don't we? Work brings many challenges. Financial worries can stretch you. Relationships aren't easy. Health comes and goes. Kids don't come with a manual. And this world is ever-changing.

In the Israelites' case, after God rained down hail and caused the sun to stand still, they were ready to return to their camp at Gilgal (Joshua 10:15). But before they could put up their feet and catch a breather, Joshua received intel that there was more work to be done. Five kings escaped and were hiding in a cave, and some enemy warriors were trying to flee to their hometowns. *Time to get back out there.*

This was the Lord's battle, yes, but the Israelites still had to go—and you're called to keep pressing the enemy back, **and dare I say, to break a sweat too**. In the marathon of life, with twists and turns that will test your faith, stamina, commitment, and discipline, we've got to come to terms with this. Otherwise, when the battle keeps raging and the race feels never-ending, we'll misunderstand the trail blazed for us and fall into disillusionment. *Is God ever gonna save us?*

No, like the Israelites, you're called to the battlefield because it's the way to victory. It's the path to the promise. It's the means to seize what God is giving you. It's the route to the land of blessing. There's more work to be done, so we gotta suit up, keep running, and "don't stop" (Joshua 10:19, NIV). Then we, too, can declare, "I have fought the good fight, I have finished the race, I have kept the faith" (2 Timothy 4:7, NIV).

TAKE THE NEXT STEP

How does your life feel like a run versus a walk?

Jesus was able to endure and not lose sight of where He was headed because of “the joy set before him” (Hebrews 12:2, NIV). Keep your own eyes fixed on that future joy. Allow His example to “shoot adrenaline into your souls” (Hebrews 12:3, MSG).

50

Stomp to Get Your Stomping Ground

Joshua 10:17-27

What is the biggest unknown to you at this very moment?

As I'm writing this, we finally have a lead on a piece of land. After years of praying for our next home and meeting nothing but dead ends, we signed a purchase agreement, but . . . there's a little caveat that allows the sellers to take it back at any point. So here I sit, twiddling my thumbs in uncertainty. **Fun, right?**

However, by the time this book is printed and in your hands, we'll know how the story panned out. If it goes our way, we'll already have moved in, and if you follow me on social media, you'll know the answer to this question mark of the past.

This is how it is with Bible stories too. With future chapters a mere flip ahead, we know how the stories play out. But the people living through them didn't have this privilege. The Israelites had to *live their lives in faith* amid the unknowns, the uncharted territory, the mystery.

Here's one thing they couldn't have known: Makkedah (where the five escaped kings were hiding) was the royal Canaanite city at the time, but it would someday be assigned to the tribe of Judah.[9] **Seeing what I'm seeing?** This enemy-held territory would turn into the Israelites' *home*.

To God, this was no question mark. The current tenants had violated their lease by dismissing the Landlord, and God had armed Joshua with the eviction notice. What was condemned property would soon be renovated and become the dominion of God's people.

But it would only be their stomping ground if they would stomp on their enemies.

Sometimes, we view the unknown as if the possibility of losing or failing is still in play. But again, what if the battle isn't meant to pose that question? What if in God's eyes, the victory is already secured? That would mean the current fight doesn't put our future in jeopardy—it's merely the means of reclaiming enemy-held territory that, in Christ, already rightfully belongs to us.

Just as Joshua called forth his commanders to "put your feet on the necks of these kings" for "this is what the LORD will do to all the enemies you are going to fight" (Joshua 10:24-25, NIV), God has placed all things under Jesus' feet (Ephesians 1:22). Equipped with His power, "you will tread down the wicked, for they will be ashes under the soles of your feet on the day which I am preparing" (Malachi 4:3, NASB).

In the life paid for by Christ, you have already been given peace. You've inherited a spirit of power, love, and a sound mind (2 Timothy 1:7). God wants you to dwell in unity, hope, and promise. All of these things can be your God-given territory. But to seize it, He is summoning you to stomp on the neck of Satan and his agents. It's up to you: In the face of the unknown, let's go forward today and *do exactly that.*

Go all in because it's all yours.

TAKE THE NEXT STEP

What is the enemy-held territory that rightfully belongs to you in Christ? How can you stomp on the neck of your opposition and claim that land?

Remember what God's Word says about your enemies: "Being made Christ's footstool . . . they are also made [yours]."[10] Move forward and claim your home sweet home.

EN ROUTE TO THE NEXT BATTLE, remember . . .

1. Stop in your tracks + give thanks to Jesus
2. The One in you is greater than the one in the world
3. Consult the Lord for wisdom on how to proceed
4. In Christ, you aren't the victim, but the victor
5. Interpret any threat as a cue to press in + expand the territory of your victory
6. When your energy is zapped, His strength will carry you on
7. Boldly pray "sun stand still" prayers
8. Realize there's more at play than just what you see
9. Life is a marathon in which you're called to endure
10. In Christ, today's battlefield is tomorrow's stomping ground

MILEPOST 6

Finish Strong

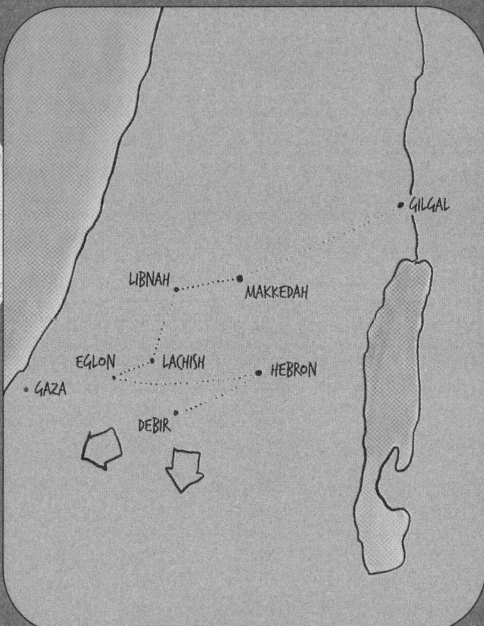

Whether it's the beginning, middle, or end, we all dislike some part of every process. **Where's the rub for you?**

Maybe you tend to start books only to lose steam midway through (**unlike this one, though, right?**).

Or maybe it's the finishing and you also let piles of leaves sit in your yard, killing the grass underneath, like someone in our household who will remain unnamed…(although he is very cute).

I'm the exact opposite. Growing up, my mom kept telling me to clean my room and I didn't—until she started piling my clothes in one part of my room. None the wiser, I'd pick it up from there. I guess all I needed was the push to begin.

Over these next ten days of following the Israelites, we will see how important each part of the process was to seizing the Promised Land.

Every step mattered.

Every battle held purpose.

And every victory expanded their claim on the God-given territory.

If they had stayed on the other side of the Jordan, they never would've known the land overflowing with milk and honey. If they had stopped at Jericho, they would've missed out on controlling the valley of the southern country. And if they had grown complacent in the central region, they would've forgone the monumental high of reaching the hills in the northern country.

The same is true in our lives. God is sending us out with a purpose, and every season matters. So let's not tread lightly—He is preparing you for what He's prepared *for* you.

It's time to finish strong.

51

The Zigzags Will Someday Make Sense

Joshua 10:28-39

Ever play the board game Life? Classic, right?

My kids are INTO IT right now, and you know what I've found? Sometimes, I do draw the Fashion Designer card that I wanted all along. I have as many kids as available spots in my car. And the coveted mansion fits into my budget when I land on the "buy a house" space.

But other times, I receive the lowest salary offered—while my seven-year-old daughter somehow makes six figures . . . **honestly, what gives?** Or I spin a number that requires me to pay for damages from a house fire, legal fees due to a lawsuit, and even replacement costs for stolen belongings. **(A little too real for family game night if you ask me.)** Adding insult to injury, these unfortunate events also force my car backwards on the board, to squares I thought I was well past.

Such is *actual* life though, right? Sometimes, things do go our way. We marry our high school or college sweetheart. We have the average 1.94 children as scheduled. And we have enough in the bank to build that dream house.

Other times, the car breaks down. Infertility delays the start of your family. A job loss sets you back. You're not as far along as you'd like and nowhere near the success level of your friends.

The Israelites followed their own path of life.

Immediately after treading on the necks of the enemy kings, "Joshua captured and destroyed the town of Makkedah. He killed everyone in it, including the king, leaving no survivors" (Joshua 10:28). Skim through the rest of the chapter, and it's like *Groundhog Day* but without Bill Murray. They booked it to the next town, attacked, and destroyed everything and everyone. Next city—lather, rinse, repeat.

If you follow this swift raid on a map though, it doesn't appear like their warpath held any rhyme or reason. Just one big zigzag.

But take a look at each stop, and we see that Joshua's attacks targeted the key cities. Libnah, with its towering cliffs connecting the Judean highlands with the Philistine plain, would only be advantageous. Lachish, which was likely the strongest city among the allied cities of Lachish, Eglon, and Hebron, would surely prove helpful. Eglon, bordering the Philistines on the high road from Gaza to Jerusalem and controlling the valley, would no doubt be strategic. And Hebron, at the most southerly road center of the highland system, would be just as tactical.[1]

All in all, while the zigzag pattern may look like nonsense, each city was key to conquering the whole region.

You may not understand today why your life has taken a sharp turn to who-knows-where. And you may not know tomorrow why you landed on that square. But truth be told, "The Lord directs the steps of the godly" (Psalm 37:23). If He has brought you to a specific place, He has a specific purpose for you to fulfill, and it's a key city you need to conquer.

So move forward—no matter if the path looks linear or you're snailing around the curves, coughing in the dust left behind by your first-grader. The fuller victory of tomorrow depends on the smaller victories of today.

TAKE THE NEXT STEP

If you had to map out the key moments of your life, would they follow a linear trajectory, or is the progression all over the place?

Remember that God is sending you out as more than a conqueror (Romans 8:37). Let that promise shift your perspective.

52

He's Sending You Too

Joshua 10:40-43

Take inventory of your recent thoughts: What seems to be dominating your life these days? What's taken up residence in your mind, commanding your attention? What is the driving force behind your emotions, reactions, and decisions?

Some of us like to live in the gray (**hello, parenthood without one-size-fits-all solutions**), but let's think black-and-white for a moment. If you had to categorize this certain *thing* that's occupying your thoughts, would you say it's good or bad?

In the Israelites' journey, they ping-ponged between the southern Canaanite cities until they conquered the whole region "in a single campaign, for the LORD, the God of Israel, was fighting for his people" (Joshua 10:42).

Notice: The Israelites didn't instigate this fight on a whim, merely looking to stir up trouble or greedily wanting more. Rather, "this conquest took place 1) at the command of the Lord and 2) through His power."[2]

In other words, it was God's idea. It was His timing, and it was by His authority.

No less than with the Israelites, some opposition is claiming squatting rights on your God-given territory, too, and it's time for it to go. God sees this enemy with its fear, discouragement, and despair wreaking havoc in your life and chipping away at your faith, joy, and hope. He will no longer stand for it.

Why? Jesus did not come to this earth, go through the pain and work of the cross, and rise again in victory just so you could continue to be taunted by the enemy He has already defeated. He did not endure suffering just so the evil rulers and authorities and powers of darkness could freely roam the land of your life, dominating you still today (Ephesians 6:12).

No, just like God commanded Joshua and His people to fight this enemy, He requires the same of us . . . at His command and by His power.

The obstacles may be bigger. The threat scarier. And the fight requiring more of you than you have left. But God didn't tell Joshua, "Go to battle! I'll be up here, so report back when you're done. Good luck!"

Far from it. God was on the battlefield "fighting for his people" (Joshua 10:42). It was by His strength, might, and sovereignty that they won, and it's by the same that you'll see the victory in your life too.

TAKE THE NEXT STEP

Map out your own campaign. In what areas of your life do you need to march forth and "take up the sword of the Spirit" (Ephesians 6:17)?

Rest in God's promises and hear His word for you: "Go in the strength you have. . . . Am I not sending you?" (Judges 6:14, NIV). He is with you every step of the way.

53

When Your Past Comes at You Again

Joshua 11:1-3

"Leave the past in the past" is such a nice sentiment, isn't it? Just move on from that broken relationship! Let go of that grief and heartache! Turn the page on your past mistakes, and start a new chapter!

We'd love to, but then . . . that past keeps haunting us. The deep scars continue to mess with our present. The memories come back in living color. And the consequences are still sending ripple effects into the future.

So what now?

After the Israelites defeated the southern kingdom of Canaan, they turned their eyes north. This would be the last major area to conquer, and they received their marching orders. Yet these northern kings were not cut from the same cloth as their southern counterparts. They would not so easily roll over and play dead. They were much stronger. More strategic. And had much more at their disposal.

In fact, King Jabin of Hazor, the head honcho of the northern kings, sent a call to arms to his subordinate rulers. And sure enough, "all these kings came out to fight. Their combined armies formed a vast horde. And with all their horses and chariots, they covered the landscape like the sand on the seashore" (Joshua 11:4).

Before we pick up our sword and join the battle cry, it's worth noting that while these other kings reported to King Jabin, his supervisor was none other than the Pharaoh in Egypt.[3] To add coals to the fire, the last time the Israelites had chariots charging at them, a Pharaoh had led the charge. He came out with "six hundred of the best chariots, along with all the other chariots of Egypt, with officers over all of them" (Exodus 14:7, NIV) in hopes of enslaving God's people once again.

Make no mistake: Your current battle may have a connection to your past too.

Your mistrust of others today stems from your abandonment yesterday.

Your fear originates from bad news delivered in the past.

Your trial is linked to prior opposition.

The Pharaoh you thought you had escaped and put behind you long ago is rearing its ugly head anew, wanting once again to take you down and be your master.

Don't panic. Don't give up. You are armed and equipped for this battle. You stand as "a good soldier of Christ Jesus" (2 Timothy 2:3) with the Lord Almighty as Commander. You're covered head to toe in protective armor, and using God's mighty weapons, you have all the "divine power to destroy strongholds" (Ephesians 6:10-17; 2 Corinthians 10:4, ESV).

So when that old slave driver comes at you again, with new tactics to get you under its thumb, remember you're already "under God's mighty hand" (1 Peter 5:8, NIV), and neither you nor I are going back to Egypt. For "if the Son sets you free, you are truly free" (John 8:36), and ain't *nothing* gonna reverse that status.

TAKE THE NEXT STEP

What past circumstances still affect your life today?

Instead of allowing them to paralyze you or instigate fear, flip your interpretation to propel you forward and bolster your faith. Remember Galatians 5:1: "It is for freedom that Christ has set us free. Stand firm, then, and do not let yourselves be burdened again by a yoke of slavery" (NIV).

54

Do Not Fear, Say What?

Joshua 11:6

Where do you feel outnumbered or outmatched?

I'll always remember sitting across the desk from my oncologist upon our first meeting. He pulled out a packet listing potential risks if I were to move forward with chemotherapy and radiation. First, summarizing short-term threats, he mentioned loss of muscle movement in my neck, a depletion in my egg supply, or early menopause leaving me unable to have kids. He then outlined long-term hazards—breast cancer being a common second cancer that could come in my thirties, as well as heart attack or cardiac arrest in my forties.

Suffice it to say, I felt in over my head. To this day, the opposition seems bigger than I can handle. And the odds don't always seem that great either.

If you're facing an uphill battle too, with the odds stacked against you, the future overwhelming you, and the opposition causing you to despair, you'll love counting the heads of the Israelite's northern opponents. They included the kings of Madon, Shimron, Acshaph; "all the kings of the northern hill country; the kings in the Jordan Valley south of Galilee; the kings in the Galilean foothills; the kings of

Naphoth-dor on the west; the kings of Canaan, both east and west; the kings of the Amorites, the Hittites, the Perizzites, the Jebusites in the hill country, and the Hivites . . . on the slopes of Mount Hermon" (Joshua 11:1-3).

It's a long list, and "it is precisely in reading this extended, detailed, particularizing description of Israel's opposition that you begin to feel how overwhelming the enemy is, to sense in line-upon-line fashion the almost hopeless situation Israel faces."[4] You and I are not the only ones up against something far greater than ourselves. Here Joshua was, confronting Hazor, which was probably the largest city of Palestine in Bible times and had 300,000 infantrymen, 10,000 cavalry riders, and 20,000 chariots.[5] Meaning Joshua was about to face perhaps the greatest battle of his life.

Yet with it all culminating here, what does God say to our leading man? "Do not be afraid of them" (Joshua 11:6). **Lemme give my CliffsNotes on this phrase:**

1. It's one of God's most-used sayings. How encouraging is our reassuring God?
2. It's never used when the victory is clear. Rather, it's said "when there seemed to be genuine cause for fear."[6] Wherever *you* feel fear, know God is equally letting you know that you still have nothing to fear. He has a handle on it.
3. It isn't just a nice suggestion, but a *command*. No matter how overpowering the claws of fear may feel, we *can* master it and cast it off—because our Master is its master, and it's already been defeated.

Ultimately, we, too, can resist the spirit of fear by calling on the Spirit of God *every time*.

TAKE THE NEXT STEP

What big battle do you face? Which of the three points above stands out most to you?

Hear the Word of the Lord afresh today: “Do not be afraid. . . . By this time tomorrow I will hand all of them over to Israel as dead men” (Joshua 11:6). Surely victory is ahead for you too.

55

Trust in ______ or Trust in God?

Joshua 11:6-9

How are you tempted to fill in that ⬆ blank?

I'll admit it. Every time I see a new symptom in myself or my family, I face the same tug-of-war: Run straight to MyChart to schedule a doctor appointment, or run to the Lord in prayer first.

Hear me out: I know God has blessed physicians with knowledge that I do not have, so it's not at all wrong to seek their counsel, and I usually do. But I hear a warning in the final incrimination of King Asa. After developing a serious foot disease, this king "did not seek the LORD's help but turned only to his physicians" (2 Chronicles 16:12). Showing who I turn to *first* and *only* matters—**because that's who I trust most to help me, right?**

In the same way, chariots were the most advanced weapon in Joshua's day, and only the most powerful nations had them. Seen as the linchpin of any battle, they not only carried two soldiers—one driving, the other wielding a weapon—they were also "armed with iron hooks . . . to cut down men as they drove along."[7] Compared to the Israelite warriors on foot with mere swords in their hands, the northern Canaanite armies held quite the advantage.

But what's interesting is that these chariots were disassembled, carried over hills to the battle site, and then reassembled with plenty of time to spare before the action started.

Or at least that was the plan.

Instead, Joshua led the Israelites into battle sooner than the northern kings expected. Their chariots were still disassembled, leveling the playing field.[8] You'd *think* it would be strategic to swipe this advanced weaponry as plunder, right? But God commanded, "You must cripple their horses and burn their chariots" (Joshua 11:6).

Say what? Doesn't this seem like a waste? Wouldn't (literally) more horsepower have been helpful for future warfare? Yet God wasn't interested in His people picking up the enemy's weapons. Likewise, today, the world attacks with its tongue and silences with its judgment, and God doesn't want us to pick up these bad habits either—but to "do everything with love" (1 Corinthians 16:14).

Also notice that God's instruction wasn't to *kill* the horses but to hamstring them. As in, they would be effectively crippled in warfare, yes, but they could still be used for domestic purposes (**and OFC, to pet**). What the enemy aims to use against us today, God will flip for our advantage as well.

Above all else, burning these chariots was a matter of the heart. "Some trust in chariots and some in horses, but we trust in the name of the Lord our God" (Psalm 20:7, ESV). Instead of depending on military strength, fuzzy pets, and worldly weapons, God's people then **and now** are called to rely on the Lord. When we do, we'll find He's sturdier, greater, and more powerful than any horse or chariot could ever prove to be.

TAKE THE NEXT STEP

Fill in the blank with what you see around you: Some trust in ______________ and others ______________, but I will trust in the name of the Lord my God.

Another translation says, "We will remember the name of the Lord our God" (NKJV). How can you remember His Name first and foremost today?

56

Bigger Battle, Bigger Victory

Joshua 11:10-15

Remember when I thought I was dying, but as it happens, my colon was only leading an internal revolt, becoming annoyingly intolerant of all foods I consider delightful? Well, my doctor recommended I test out a low-FODMAP diet to figure out which foods were triggering the most trouble.

Reporting back: Turns out this diet is extremely restrictive—and **particularly lame** when the rest of your family gorges on ice cream and pizza right in front of your face.

Pouring oil on the flames, this happened around Mother's Day, when my daughter's class was filling out the typical mother questionnaire. While other kids answered "mom's favorite drink" with coffee or wine, Hazel filled in Prune Juice. Of course, everyone's answers were stapled together and sent home for *all* moms to read at their earliest enjoyment. So now the entire class of 2031 is aware Heidi Lee Anderson's drink of choice matches their great-grandma's. **#thisis30**

But here's the point: By eliminating most foods and then slowly reintroducing them, I ended up making great strides and covering more ground.

Who woulda thought Joshua and IBS had so much in common?

In contrast to how he previously overtook cities battle by battle, our guy was able to conquer the northern kingdoms in one major blow because they had made a singular alliance. With this sole showdown near Merom, "Joshua conquered the entire region—the hill country, the entire Negev, the whole area around the town of Goshen, the western foothills, the Jordan Valley, the mountains of Israel, and the Galilean foothills" (Joshua 11:16).

Some battles in your own life will be like that too. The bigger they are, the more territory you conquer at once.

Others will look more like individual, smaller conquests . . . and that's okay too. They're still a piece of the Promised Land, and each victory moves you forward.

What's noteworthy IMO is that God didn't send Joshua to this larger battle first. Not even when they next stood at a crossroads in the central region since God directed them south. It wasn't until those past battles were under their belt that they were prepared for this much bigger fight.

God knows what *you* can and cannot handle too, and in due time, He wants to enlarge your territory. He wants you to seize all of the Promised Land. He wants you to dwell in the land overflowing with milk and honey. But how you respond in these smaller territories will affect how you respond in the face of much larger ones.

Make no mistake: He's preparing you for what He's prepared *for* you and given you the exact measure of grace and strength you need at every stop. So move ahead in the battle—big or small—knowing it's not meant to tear you down but only to build you up "and give you an inheritance with all those he has set apart for himself" (Acts 20:32).

TAKE THE NEXT STEP

What smaller battles have strengthened your faith? How have larger battles expanded your trust and confidence in God?

James 1:3-4 says, "When your faith is tested, your endurance has a chance to grow. So let it grow, for when your endurance is fully developed, you will be perfect and complete, needing nothing." Key word: *let*.

57

Don't Give Up in the Middle . . . Your Victory Is Coming

Joshua 11:16-18

Waiting is the absolute worst, isn't it?

I'm not just talking about the whoppers like waiting for your house to sell, for your spouse to land a job after losing the old one, or for a positive pregnancy test after a miscarriage. Those are lame, **no question about it**.

But even those days when you hit all the red lights, the drive-through is backed up, your toddler decides to dress herself when you're already running late, and your phone isn't loading because the connection is slow . . . *painful*, is it not?

The Israelites waited a long time to get where they were now. Their parents and grandparents had to extend their wilderness stay for forty years. And even now, it wasn't like the second the Israelites stepped into the Promised Land, they could unroll their welcome mats and settle right in to neighborhood block parties.

No, we've followed their footsteps for fifty-seven days now. We watched as they waited in faith for walls to come down, as they climbed hills and trudged through valleys, and as they constantly confronted enemy armies.

It was a grind to get here. And while it was only two months and eleven chapters for *us*, they had to wage war "for a long time to accomplish this" (Joshua 11:18). This "long time" to seize the land totaled about seven years.[9]

Battles take *time*. We may wish for the quick microwave solution. We may hope to find the Roku remote of life and fast-forward through the boring and hard parts. And we may still prefer the freeway over the roundabout back roads, moving at a snail's pace through our circumstances.

But if there's one thing we've heard from God time and time again, it's to not become discouraged in long-suffering. He is with you, He has a purpose, and He gets the final word.

In other words, in Christ, **victory is always a-comin'**.

And now we come to the day when the Israelites see this for themselves. The conquest is *finally complete*. There are still cities to conquer and pockets of resistance to overcome, sure. But the land of Canaan—from the northern kingdom, to the central kingdom, and all the way down to the southern kingdom—is now Israelite territory.

They made it! Mission accomplished. **Home sweet home**.

In your own struggles, you may feel tired from the fight. The battles have chiseled away at your hope. You may not see any indication of victory around the corner.

But remember: There's a chapter 11 for your story too. Hold on to that when you face the raging waters of chapter 3 or the defeat of chapter 7. Hang on to hope when the deceit of chapter 9 pushes you to your breaking point.

God is still working all things together for the good of those who love Him, who are called according to His purpose (Romans 8:28). ***You, too, will see it with your own eyes***.

TAKE THE NEXT STEP

Look back on the footprints of your life. What chapter would you consider yourself in right now?

Stay faithful in the long-suffering, knowing that it "produces perseverance; perseverance, character; and character, hope" (Romans 5:3, NIV). "And this hope will not lead to disappointment. For we know how dearly God loves us, because he has given us the Holy Spirit to fill our hearts with his love" (verses 4-5, NLT).

58

Black Hearts Turned White as Snow

Joshua 11:19-20

Who was the guinea pig in your family?

You know who I'm talking about. Your parents weren't parents until that kid was born. They didn't know what rules to make until that kid needed them. They didn't choose their method of discipline until that kid pushed the boundaries. And they didn't know what mistakes to learn from until they made them . . . with **that kid.**

Ty and I just admitted to Oscar that he's our guinea pig. So much of how we parent our younger kids was gleaned from trial and error with him as our oldest. But one thing that worked with him and that I've carried forward with my girls is when I catch them lying or saying something hurtful, I gasp. Trying to explain its heavy significance, I'll say, "That's the kind of stuff that turns your heart black!"

Jury's still out whether this approach will have them seeking therapy in later days. Even so, I haven't found a better way to paint the mental picture that when they sin, they're not living in *life* but choosing *death.* They're not acting as children of light but participating in darkness. And it matters—to their freedom, to the state of others' souls, and to their God.

Case in point with the Canaanites. God wanted to restore blessing to these families through Abraham (Genesis 12:3). For *four hundred years,* He waited for them to repent and receive this blessing. But they chose to sacrifice their children instead of giving a "sacrifice of praise" (Hebrews 13:15). They chose to take advantage of temple prostitutes' bodies instead of offering their own bodies to God as a living sacrifice, pure and pleasing (Romans 12:1). And they chose to "[worship] and [serve] the things God created instead of the Creator himself" (Romans 1:25). Ultimately, because "no one in this region made peace with the Israelites except the Hivites of Gibeon. . . . All the others were defeated" (Joshua 11:19).

But notice the fate of those who chose the opposite. Rahab, the prostitute spared from her city's destruction because she chose faith in God. The Gibeonites, an entire city protected because they chose allegiance to God and His people.

This has always been God's heart: He wants *all* people to be saved and to come to a knowledge of the truth (1 Timothy 2:4). He wants *all* to return to Him, being "slow to anger and abounding in love, and he *relents* from sending calamity" (Joel 2:13, NIV, italics added). "He does not want anyone to be destroyed, but wants everyone to repent" (2 Peter 3:9).

But He will not force anyone to love Him. To obey Him. To return to Him as much as He wholeheartedly wants it.

Good news, though, for anyone who takes Him up on His offer: "I will give you a new heart and put a new spirit in you; I will remove from you your heart of stone and give you a heart of flesh" (Ezekiel 36:27, NIV). By putting His Spirit in us, He takes our black hearts and makes them white as snow (Isaiah 1:18). It's up to us: Will we or will we not make peace with God? **All of heaven hopes we say yes.**

TAKE THE NEXT STEP

Do you know someone who's hardened their heart toward God?

Never stop praying for them, and be encouraged that God is "wonderfully kind, tolerant, and patient," hoping to lead them to repentance (Romans 2:4). Keep putting Jesus on display!

59

Grasshoppers in Us vs. Grasshoppers to Him

Joshua 11:21-23

What giants are casting their shadows over you today? What's the challenge, obstacle, or struggle towering over you, seeming far bigger than you could fight in your own strength?

Is it that mountain of debt blocking your peace?

Is it the giant of health concerns that overshadows your joy?

Is it a relationship, a hiccup in your career path, or the loss of a loved one that darkens the sky no matter how brightly the sun shines?

For a season, it seemed a black cloud followed me around every day. No matter how hard I prayed or how long I waited for it to blow over, I couldn't escape its gloom.

But the day came when I remembered the Creator God I serve "covers the heavens with clouds; he prepares rain for the earth; he makes grass grow on the hills" (Psalm 147:8, ESV). It was suddenly obvious to me that (1) even the black cloud hovering over my life has to answer to His command; (2) a cloudy forecast cannot darken my day when the Son is my Light and He tells the clouds which way to go; (3) if the cloud is a means of bringing the rain, I best prepare to see growth and new life shoot up as a result; and (4) that black cloud is *nothing to Him* and will be used for His purposes.

I imagine this is how the Israelites felt as they faced the Anakites, since these descendants of Anak had cost their parents the Promised Land. When Moses sent spies to scope out Canaan, the majority came back quaking in their boots over these people. "The land we traveled through and explored will devour anyone who goes to live there," they said. "We even saw giants there, *the descendants of Anak*. Next to them we felt like grasshoppers" (Numbers 13:32-33, italics added).

Now it was up to the Israelites: Would they follow the retreating footsteps of their parents or press forward and seize the promise of God?

"God sits above the circle of the earth. The people below seem like grasshoppers *to him*!" (Isaiah 40:22, italics added). Sure, the parents of the promise may have felt like grasshoppers compared to the Anakites, but these giants looked like mere grasshoppers to their God.

The same is true with the giants we face. They may look scary. They may be bigger and stronger than us. But when have we ever stood alone? God promises to be with us, to help us, to uphold us (Isaiah 41:10). Our problems are nothing but puny insects under His feet, and He is more than capable of repelling them. Instead of retreating in fear, let's assume His vantage point and **press forward in faith**.

TAKE THE NEXT STEP

How can you reframe your view of the giants in your life through the perspective of God's eyes?

God's Word says that "nothing is too hard for [Him]" and all of heaven and earth is under His great power and outstretched arm (Jeremiah 32:17). Let this truth embolden your prayers despite any lingering fears.

60

What Time Is It?

Joshua 11:21-23

What time is it?

I don't mean literally, like 8:13 p.m. CST. **Although, since I do often misplace my phone, I tend to ask that question repeatedly.** But I'm wondering what *season* the Lord has you in.

I was just getting into the groove of podcasting, enjoying season 1 of *Trade a Lie for a Truth*. I was also creating new posts on social media. Additionally, we were listing our house, which meant cleaning, landscaping, and painting. And the due date for this manuscript was looming—along with the end of the school year, which meant my kids would soon be home **all day, e'ry day**.

I was still tempted to do it all. Edit and launch new weekly episodes. Post on Instagram daily. Whip this house into shape. Crank out a best-selling devotional. Be a present, fun mom. And you know, keep working out, making homemade meals, and scheduling speaking engagements. Oh yeah, plus, be a good wife and launch a new small group!

Couldn't be that hard, right?

Until the mere thought of this to-do list felt like a noose around my neck. I was gently reminded by Ty that all of the above should be fun and enjoyable—not to mention, *optional* and of my own choosing!

I was convicted that if truly "for everything there is a season, a time for every activity under heaven" (Ecclesiastes 3:1), why was I trying to pack everything into this one season as if it was my one and only chance? I prayed for wisdom: *God, what activity do you have for me now? What's my best yes? What is my current season* actually for*?*

For the Israelites, it was no longer a time of war. It was a time of rest (Joshua 11:23). It was time to relax in the land they worked so hard to seize. It was time to enjoy the special inheritance God had given them.

For you, is it time to break down or a time to build up?

A time to tear or a time to mend?

A time to keep, a time to gather, or a time to throw away?

A time to search or a time to give up?

A time to plant, a time to uproot, or a time to harvest?

A time to grieve or a time to dance?

A time for war or a time for peace?

What time do you feel the Lord leading you to? I'm not asking what time you *wish* it to be . . . **(I always want it after 10 a.m., no doubt.)** But there are some things in this season that need our focus, which means there are some things in this season we must step away from. Next season, it may be totally different, and He may be setting aside certain things for later. But *this season* is indeed precious, and God has something for us that we don't want to miss.

TAKE THE NEXT STEP

Read the list in Ecclesiastes 3:1-8, then ask the Lord, *What time is it for me? What do you want me to do in this season?*

Like the Israelites, rest today in the land He's given you.

FINISHING STRONG
travel tips

1. Fuller victory tomorrow depends on smaller victories today
2. The enemies claiming squatting rights are no longer tolerated by the Landlord nor you
3. Reflect on past triumphs to fuel today's confidence
4. Drive out the spirit of fear by calling on the Spirit of God

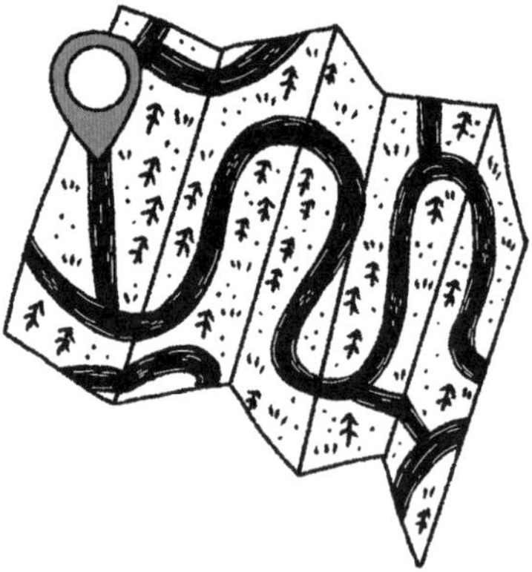

5. Trust in the Lord vs. the things of this world
6. He's preparing you for what He's prepared for you
7. Battles take time, but in Christ, victory is always a-comin'
8. God wants all people to be saved, so take Him up on the offer of peace
9. Our giants are nothing but puny grasshoppers under God's feet
10. Ask God what season you're in + live out that purpose

MILEPOST 7

Post-Battle Analysis

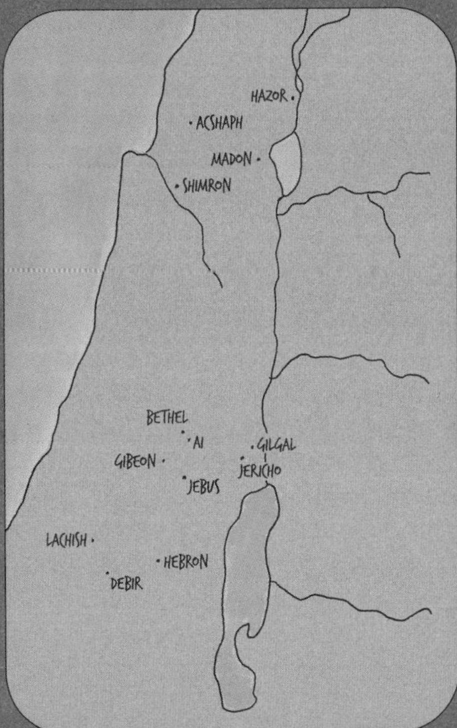

There are two types of people: those who don't make lists, and those who add what they've already done to their to-do list just so they can check it off . . . Who are you?

I am, and will forever be, the latter. Not giving up that serotonin boost **FO' NUTTIN'**.

But whether or not you excessively make lists, we're about to travel through my favorite portion of Joshua's journey, and trust me, it will NOT let you down. As our man looks back at all God had brought His people through, we'll see ten important pieces to mine out in our own post-battle analysis.

The discoveries God has in store for us are rich.

The truths are absolutely freeing.

And the future implications are mind-blowing.

We would be wise to follow such a debrief not just once but regularly. After every trial and every win, we can stop. Reflect. And make this list to take inventory of these ten things before we plow ahead into the next phase, problem, or prayer request.

"Let your roots grow down into him, and let your lives be built on him. Then your faith will grow strong in the truth you were taught, and you will overflow with thankfulness" (Colossians 2:7). The goods rooted and grounded in love are just ahead. In a tone that sounds very much like T Swift, ***are you ready for it?***

61

Victory Roll Call

Joshua 12:1

Think back to your battles won.

Maybe like me, past warfare on your health in the form of cancer, Lyme disease, and emergency surgeries comes to mind first. Or maybe it's a financial clash of arms due to unemployment, debt, or unforeseen bills. Possibly a fight against injustice? Or strife within your marriage, with your kids, or in a particular relationship that you met head-on and now stand in triumph over today.

What if you made a list of each trial overcome? My MIL keeps a health journal, and since I've seen double-digits of doctor appointments in merely a month's time, this was a good idea for me too. As I've pressed into current battles, this recounting of past conquests strengthens my confidence that my Savior still saves.

As the Israelites are now able to rest in the Promised Land, it's time for them to also conduct a post-battle analysis. Line by line, Joshua lists all "the kings of the land whom the Israelites had defeated" (Joshua 12:1, NIV).

Why? What's the point? By looking back, we see these important truths:

God keeps His word. Just like He had *already given* the Israelites this land before they even set foot on it, "the One who calls you is [still] faithful" (1 Thessalonians 5:24, NIV). What He has for you is *for you*, and you're gonna live to sink your toes into that Land of Promise.

God's success rate builds confidence. The Israelites could realize that if God was faithful *then*, He's gonna be faithful *again*. There are over three thousand promises in His Word, and they are all "Yes" in Christ (2 Corinthians 1:20). You will see Him make good on *every promise*, **one hundred percent chance, without fail.**

God grows fruit from obedience. The battle lost can at times be directly tied to disobedience, but on the flip side, we reap the benefits God has promised when we obey His Word. He chose you to "go and bear fruit—fruit that will last" (John 15:16, NIV), but that only comes from abiding in the Vine.

God desires total victory for you. When Jesus said, "It is finished" (John 19:30), He meant *it is finished*. Every enemy defeated, sting of death gone, sins forgiven, debt paid, victory sure. "Like Joshua, he left nothing undone"[1] and wants you to press through any partial fulfillment and seize the whole shebang.

God deserves our praise. Through the abundant life in Christ, God is bringing you into a land where "nothing is lacking" (Deuteronomy 8:9), and He wants you to eat your fill. But then, "be sure to praise the LORD your God for the good land he has given you" (verse 10).

What do you say we make our own post-battle analysis? Let's consider the past battles won and dust for divine fingerprints. As we count our blessings, our faith, praise, and confidence will inevitably grow.

TAKE THE NEXT STEP

Which of the five points stand out most to you?

62

Are You Missing This on Your List?

Joshua 12:2-6

When you take a selfie with others and then pull it up, what's the first thing you look at?

Lemme guess . . . *you*, right? (I know you because I know me.) And if we look good, it's like, *Got the shot!* Doesn't matter if our spouse is half-blinking. **Win some, lose some.** No matter if a kid's picking their nose or having a meltdown. **What do people expect with four kids, anyways?** And even if your friend wants a retake, it's like, "Yeah, sure." ***(But we both know which one we're gonna post . . .)***[2]

Pastor Jason Strand puts it this way, "There's nothing wrong with looking at yourself in a picture. But it is symptomatic of how self-focused we can be."[3]

What I find both interesting and convicting is that, even in Joshua's post-battle analysis, our guy isn't recounting the kings and territories defeated solely under *his* command. No, the victories he lists first (Joshua 12:2-5) were won under *Moses'* leadership.

As in, Joshua couldn't have gotten to where he stood without the prior work of Moses, and he knew it. It was a tag-team effort, a domino effect across generations. Moses' legacy was the springboard for Joshua to reach total victory.

What are the hard-fought battles *our* predecessors have won for us?

Whether parents, grandparents, mentors, or pastors, what skirmishes have *they* fought so we wouldn't have to?

As we list battles won, let's take a cue from Joshua and not just zero in on our own triumphs. Let's add those won by our forerunners too. When we look outside of ourselves, not only does our gratitude swell and our praise multiply, but we realize what's at stake for future generations as well.

For those who conquered the Promised Land in faith and continued to dwell there in obedience, we'll see blessing upon their children and their children's children. But for those who forfeited their territories to the remaining Canaanites and chose lives of disobedience instead, we'll see the opposite effect ripple out. Likewise, our actions have consequences for those coming after us.

It all comes down to choice though. We won't just stumble into one or the other—obedience and blessing, or disobedience and consequence. Both paths are taken with intention, and which step you take is up to you.

So what do you say? Your decision today doesn't have to be the same one you made yesterday. Let's set the course of resolute faith and fight the good fight, knowing our freedom will have a snowball effect on generations to come.

TAKE THE NEXT STEP

What kind of legacy do you want to live today and leave tomorrow?

Take a look at your list, and beyond battles won, remember those who have gone before you too. Be spurred on by their obedience and follow their commitment in fighting on behalf of future generations.

63

It Means More Than You Think

Joshua 12:7-24

What does your name mean?

I remember when we researched this in grade school. My friend Sara squealed when she found "princess" beside her name, and Amanda bragged that she was "she who *must be* loved." **How fun to demand everyone's adoration, you know?**

My turn. Anticipation high, I ran my finger down the list to Heidi, holding my breath until I saw "noble." Not every girl's dream, but I guess *decent* . . . (**literally the definition**). But then Lee? "Meadow." So, like a swamp?

Cool.

When we had our own kids, I wanted to give them names they'd be proud of. On top of pulling from our family tree, we chose names with meanings that would be the talk of the third grade. Oscar means "God's spear, champion warrior," a powerful declaration as we continually place him in the hands of God. Mabel means "beautiful, loving, loveable," and created by Love, she is all those things. Hazel means "God sees," and I'm so grateful God knew this splash of joy—our rainbow baby—was coming beyond the stormy clouds. Lastly, Dottie means "gift of God," and by the smiles she gives us all, she's indeed heaven-sent.

Maybe you feel my pain because you're nothing but a "wetland," "dweller near the ash tree meadow" (Ashley), "elf ruler" (Aubrey), or "crooked nose" (Cameron)—***although let it be known you are more than that deviated nasal septum***. My point, though, is that meanings can be significant.

This is equally true for territories conquered in the Promised Land. For instance, Ai ("heap of ruins") was once the source of defeat for the Israelites but now lies in rubble—finally living up to its translation.[4] He will flip losses for *your* good too. Just humble yourself under the mighty hand of God, and in due time, He will lift you up (1 Peter 5:6).

And remember how each Canaanite kingdom was described as either *devoted to* or *conquered by* God? This is key. Towns like Jerusalem ("teaching of peace")[5] and Adullam ("justice of the people")[6] certainly *belong* to God: The ways to peace and justice are devoted to Him alone.

Other kingdoms, like Jarmuth ("heights"),[7] remind me that *nothing*—neither height nor depth—can separate us from the love of God (Romans 8:39), and all distance was vanquished by Jesus' death and resurrection. Any "wall" (Geder)[8] meant to keep us out, we can scale with God (Psalm 18:29). And a true "fortress" (Aphek)[9] is found in Christ: "He is my shield, the power that saves me, and my place of safety" (Psalm 18:2).

God used Joshua to conquer all these things—along with thirty-one kings total!—giving the land to His people. Since it all belonged to and was devoted to Him, it would now all belong to and be devoted to His people too.

Rest assured: Our Father didn't skimp on *our* inheritance either. Indeed, our cup overflows with blessing.

TAKE THE NEXT STEP

What deeper meaning has God brought out of your past battles?

Think about how you could classify your trials as being devoted to or conquered by God. "Look, the highest heavens and the earth and everything in it all belong to the LORD your God" (Deuteronomy 10:14).

64

Time to Pass the Baton

Joshua 13:1-7

Where have you had the baton passed along to you?

Maybe it was a formal position, ministry, or business, and the leader trained you to carry on their work. Or possibly it's a tradition you continue for your family. Or maybe you pass the baton, picking up the kids after work and school before your spouse takes over, carpooling to practices and games.

In handing over control, the hope is for a smooth transition so things continue as they should, right? Just because a person isn't there doesn't mean an idea has to die or a role has to go by the wayside. And it doesn't mean the future of the Promised Land is no more.

This is where Israel is at. God promised Abraham *centuries ago* the entire land of Canaan would belong to the twelve tribes. Moses kicked off the project, settling two and a half tribes east of the Jordan. Then he handed over the reins to Joshua to oversee the battle campaign and allot the remaining tribes their own building sites.

. . . but now, when Joshua is around a hundred years old, the Lord says straight up, "You are now very old, and there are still very large areas of land to be taken over" (Joshua 13:1, NIV).

(Nothing like the Ancient of Days calling you ancient . . .)

But wait, all thirty-one kings were conquered! The backbone of

Canaanite power broken! So many battles won! Yet . . . the conquest was not complete? There were still Canaanites in the land? More towns to seize? More warfare ahead?

This could have made Joshua feel like a failure, couldn't it? Some of us can't even stand a box unchecked on our to-do list, so we can imagine his head hung in disappointment.

But here's the point: Although Israel had not yet possessed all the land, God said it was time to turn the future over to the tribes. No longer led by Joshua alone, these tribes would need to pick up the baton and finish what was started. Ultimately, this was the Lord's project, and He would certainly finish what He started. But it was time for someone else to do the work.

We, too, need the discernment to let go when our time has passed. We may not be the ones to complete everything we've started, and that's okay. We can still be sure that "He who began a good work in you *will* carry it on to completion until the day of Christ Jesus" (Philippians 1:6, NIV, italics added). If there's anything else still to be done? It's only the good work for someone else to take on.

In the end, God will see that *every* good work is finished.

TAKE THE NEXT STEP

How have you made plans for those who will follow in your footsteps?

Consider what you may need to delegate—even if projects remain unfinished (in your opinion). Do what you can to set up your kids, subordinates, and future generations well by passing the baton.

65

What Inhabitants Are We Tolerating?

Joshua 13:8-13

Have you ever done anything . . . halfway?

I'm laughing, because I once told my kids to unload the dishwasher only later to find the clean dishes on the counter. When I asked, "Why didn't you put them away?" they replied (**actually confused, y'all**), "You just told us to unload—not put away?" Around the same time, I told them to bring their folded laundry upstairs . . . only to find it sitting literally at the top of the steps.

When our heavenly Father was laying down the laws of justice and mercy to prepare His kids for the Promised Land, He was clear on the progression of responsibility: "*I* will give into your hands the people who live in the land, and *you* will drive them out before you" (Exodus 23:31, NIV, italics added). Seems like an easy trade-off for living in peace and abundance, does it not?

But as we zoom in on each territory and tribe, we see for the first time that they "did not drive out" some of the Canaanites (Joshua 13:13, NIV).

You read that right. God held up His end of the bargain. Yet the tribes east of the Jordan—Manasseh, Reuben, and Gad—drove out *some* . . . but not all. While this may not seem like the worst thing ever—maybe explained away with a "love thy neighbor" sign in their front yard?—there was something more serious at stake.

Our culture tends to think God barks out orders for no good reason. As if He exercises authority and expects people to fall in line. As though He's breathing fire and delighting in crushing those who disobey. Like He's a killjoy, out to steal our fun and stifle our freedom.

When those are literally the very things He came to give. When "the LORD is good to everyone" and "showers compassion on all his creation" (Psalm 145:9). When He has our best interests in mind and HAS the best for us.

God explained Himself clearly. Flip back to Exodus and we hear His important reason: "Do not let them live in your land or they will cause you to sin against me, because the worship of their gods *will certainly* be a snare to you" (23:33, NIV).

Wanna know what happened? Fast-forward centuries later, and these tribes were not only fully worshiping pagan gods, but they also were the *first ones* driven out of their inherited land by the Assyrians.

They could've avoided it all by listening to God in the first place, and we don't have to fall for the same trap. God still offers total victory for His people, but it's our choice whether we'll tolerate sin, self, Satan, and wayward laundry piles as inhabitants in the landscape of our lives.

No more. It's time you and I stay strong in the Lord and in the land by driving out every enemy of our soul.

Watch out, dishes.

TAKE THE NEXT STEP

What are you permitting to enter your life that could pull you away from God?

Christ offers the power to drive out all evil, but we must do the work of driving it out in Jesus' name. Let's ruthlessly push out sin and self, so we can stay strong in the Lord and in the land that rightfully belongs to us.

66

Turning Curses into Blessings

Joshua 13:14

Have you ever felt cursed? With a poor memory? A defective body? A dysfunctional family?

You're gonna love the Levites. As we swing over to their tribe and scratch our heads at their lack of title to any land, grab my hand and let's skip back to a certain crime scene in Genesis 34 for the full story.

Levi and Simeon, sons of Jacob, found out some punk had raped their sister, and they carried out quite the bloody, murderous revenge against the town. After killing every unsuspecting male, they carried off all their wealth, along with every woman and child.

Yikes . . . and we thought *our* families were crazy.

Well, in light of their rash vengeance, Jacob curses his sons: "Cursed be their anger, so fierce, and their fury, so cruel! I will scatter them in Jacob and disperse them in Israel" (Genesis 49:7, NIV).

And back to the Promised Land, this is exactly what we see for Levi's heirs. Not apportioned any land at all, they were instead scattered throughout the land, in cities within the territories of other tribes.

Spoiler: Good thing we have a God who turns curses into blessings.

In the bigger story, God took the curse of sin, brought upon us by Adam and Eve in Genesis 3, and sent the Second Adam (Jesus) to pay the price for humanity's punishment and set us free. "Christ redeemed us from the curse of the law by becoming a curse for us, for it is written: 'Cursed is everyone who is hung on a pole'" (Galatians 3:13, NIV; see also Deuteronomy 27:26).

God flipped the curse for us through Christ's death, and He did it in the Levites' story too. The Lord specifically chose these descendants of murderers to now be *His* priests, *His* representatives in the new land, *His* ambassadors to symbolize His very presence within the communities. These Levites were selected to be the ones leading worship services, taking care of the Temple when later built, and living in the area directly surrounding the Tabernacle—which housed God's very presence.

Do you see it? He redeemed them. With forty-eight cities set apart for them, along with pastures for their cattle (Numbers 35:1-8), God also provided for their every need by entitling them to part of the tithes and offerings of Israel. Ultimately, He said He gave *Himself* as their inheritance, "as he promised them" (Joshua 13:33).

Once again we see that God doesn't give us what we deserve—He gives far better. He takes what is intended to curse us and flips it for our good. Have hope today, for no matter what misfortune befalls you and paints a picture of doom ahead, He can turn it around in your story as well. For if Christ can turn the curse of our sin into the glory of His salvation, He can certainly flip everything else that follows.

TAKE THE NEXT STEP

What circumstance currently appears to be a curse for you?

Commit it to the Lord this very moment, and you can "trust in Him, and He will act" (Psalm 37:5, ESV). His blessing is coming.

67

It's Already Yours

Joshua 13:15-33

What do you want more than anything?

Peace of mind? A fulfilling career? A hopeful future, a large family, or vibrant health?

Pay close attention to the tribes of Reuben and Gad. Well before Moses even passed away, they were marching alongside their brothers and sisters, eyes set toward the Promised Land, with their "vast numbers of livestock" in tow (Numbers 32:1).

But after stepping into Jazer and Gilead, east of the Jordan, they realized these lands were "ideally suited for their flocks and herds" (Numbers 32:1). They asked Moses for permission to claim these lands, then built pens for their livestock and fortified towns for their wives and children. Then they were willing to "cross the Jordan and keep fighting until the Lord has driven out his enemies" (verse 21). Moses gave the green light, and for years, these tribes faithfully fought . . . even though they already had their inheritance.

Here's what I need you to see: You already are a coheir in Christ. As God's child, you have inherited peace, love, joy, and the other fruits of the Spirit; wisdom; victory; guidance; power; mercy; forgiveness; righteousness; truth; discernment; all your physical needs; the promise of eternity with Him, a room in the Father's house, and crowns in heaven; and so much more. All of it is yours in Jesus.

So go forth into the land ahead knowing it's already yours. You can go all in because it's all yours. C. H. Spurgeon said it best:

> In spiritual things, waive no spiritual right. Say to sin, that now mars your peace, "Peace is mine, clear out!" Say to sin, that stops your usefulness, "That usefulness is mine, I claim it: clear out!" Hivite, Jebusite, Girgashite . . . clear out of my heart and life, for holiness is mine. God, the sovereign possessor of all things, has given us our redeemed nature, to have and to hold for his glory, *and we mean to have it!* . . .
>
> If there be more holiness, put your foot on it; if there be more happiness, put your foot on it; if there be more usefulness, put your foot on it. Lay your claim to all that is put within your reach in Scripture; this is the victory that overcometh the world, and conquereth Canaan, even our faith. . . .
>
> Every place in the grace country upon which the sole of your foot shall tread is yours.[10]

Reuben and Gad lived this out. They fought, knowing it, and it's high time we do the same. Whatever battle comes, engage in the fight with full assurance you already have your plot of land, and your inheritance is already secure.

TAKE THE NEXT STEP

Where are you sent to fight—knowing in Christ the victory is already won?

Link arms with your brothers and sisters in Christ and seize the land with full confidence that there is an end date to this war. Like Gad and Reuben, you can live knowing you have everything to gain and nothing to lose, and in due time, you'll get to rest in your portion.

68

He Will Withhold NO Good Thing

Joshua 14:1-3

Ever feel like God is blessing others way more than you? Seeing their big house, successful job, carefree lifestyle, or harmonious marriage, you look at what you have and wonder if what they have is better.

When it was time to divide the land west of the Jordan among the rest of the tribes, instead of scrambling off to call first dibs on a certain plot, they remembered God's plan. He told Moses, "Be sure that the land is distributed by lot" (Numbers 26:55, NIV), so there would be no elbowing past their brother or inciting a rift within the family of God. No, the Lord would choose where each tribe dwelled.

In the same way, the Lord's inheritance is all ours in Christ, but *how* that looks, which backdrop each of our lives is set against, will be showcased differently.

Some plots were next to the Egyptians or bordering the Philistines, while others were tucked safely inside Canaan, with their brother clans protectively surrounding them. Some territories were on higher ground, with a view from the mountaintops, while others dipped into the valleys. Still others enjoyed a scenic display off the seacoast.

Regardless of *where* they were dwelling, it was all the Land of Milk and Honey. It was still overflowing with God's blessing. It was still a gift, a land picked for them to thrive in. Each tribe was equipped and empowered to drive out their particular enemies and dwell in peace.

This is true for our Christian walk as well, isn't it?

While you may not remember the last time you visited a doctor, I view MyChart like texting and talk to my doctor more than most talk to their friends. While I come from a believing family, you may not—and yet God knit you together in your specific mother's womb for a reason. While marriage feels seamless for some, you may have to work harder at yours.

I don't know where you've been planted, but hear me clear: In Christ, you're still dwelling in the Land of Promise. This is where He knows you can thrive. This is where He intends to bestow blessing. This is where you will find the joy of His presence and eternal pleasures at His right hand forevermore (Psalm 16:11). This is where the Great Shepherd will "equip you with every good thing to do His will" (Hebrews 13:21, BSB). This is where you, too, will see the goodness of the Lord in the land of the living (Psalm 27:13).

So refuse to fall into the comparison trap. Don't take the bait set by the enemy, believing God is withholding something good. Dismiss any "I wish I were somewhere else" notion, and put a stake in the ground, trading it for the truth: "To enjoy [my] work and accept [my] lot in life—this is indeed a gift from God" (Ecclesiastes 5:19).

That's the truth that will set you free.

TAKE THE NEXT STEP

What territory has God given you? Where are you discontented?

Remember, "The LORD will withhold no good thing from those who do what is right" (Psalm 84:11). If we have it, it's good for us. If we don't, it's either not good or the timing isn't right. God will not deny *anything* that is good for His kids.

69

You and I Are Ephraim and Manasseh

Joshua 14:4-5

Are you a firstborn, the middle child, or the baby of your family?

I'm the middle, which of course means I was overlooked and often neglected. **(Mom, I can hear you scoffing across the page—I'm just kidding.)** However, I'm also the firstborn daughter, so I don't necessarily fit the stereotypical middle child mold. Can't keep me from claiming middle child syndrome though, amiright?

Anyways.

Birth order is fun and informative to talk about nowadays. But in Old Testament times, the firstborn held unique rights, responsibilities, and privileges. Not only did they have priority and authority within the family, but they got the *best* of the inheritance and a *double portion.*

Of Israel's twelve sons, Reuben was the oldest, but as seen on Jerry Springer, he forfeited that right when he slept with his dad's concubine. The privilege should've then fallen to Simeon and Levi, but murdering a whole city **kinda** disqualified them. **(Like keeping up with the Kardashians, y'all.)**

Judah would've been next in line, but it seems Israel (Jacob), was over it and chose his favorite son, Joseph, to get the best and most. Taking it a step further, he adopted Joseph's two sons, Ephraim and Manasseh, as his own—which meant these grandsons would receive *twice as much* as Jacob's own sons . . . aka their uncles.

Most of us can easily put ourselves in the shoes of Reuben, Simeon, Levi, or even Judah and cock our head at the injustice: "That's just not fair!" But a word of caution: "That is not who we are in this story."[11]

You and I are not naturally born into the family of God as the Israelites were. Rather, born into sin and once enemies of God, we held no claim to His inheritance. But God loved us so much that He "decided in advance to adopt us into his own family . . . through Jesus Christ. This is what he *wanted to do*, and it gave him *great pleasure* . . . [to identify] you as his own" (Ephesians 1:5, 13, italics added).

Are you picking up what I'm putting down? You and I are adopted as God's children like Ephraim and Manasseh were adopted by Jacob.

Christ, the true Firstborn, has been entrusted with *everything* by the Father and given *all* authority in heaven and on earth (Matthew 11:27; 28:18). Now in Him, we are "heirs of God and coheirs with Christ" (Romans 8:17, BSB).

We didn't deserve this land. We weren't entitled to it. We weren't even in a position to earn it. But by the grace of God, we are now given the most and the best in Christ. **Who else needs a tissue?** *Oh man, what a friend we have in Jesus.*

TAKE THE NEXT STEP

In what areas have you felt entitled to blessing?

Let Ephraim and Manasseh's story remind you to see all that you have as the result of God's grace. "From his abundance we have all received one gracious blessing after another" (John 1:16).

70

Whose Voice Are You Listening To?

Joshua 14:6-9

How has someone else's faith (or lack thereof) affected *your* life?

My grandma immediately comes to mind. Her mom died when she was two. Her dad sent her to her aunt's home, leaving her stripped of both parents.

Fast-forward to when she was married and celebrating two miracle babies . . . only to lose them—one at ten days, the other around his one-year birthday.

Later, her husband died suddenly of cardiac arrest, and she lived another sixteen years on her own. During the COVID lockdown, she was in a memory care unit, with no visitors except at the window.

But can I tell you something? Growing up, I didn't know most of this. Until the day she died, I only knew a faith-filled grandma, who never showed an ounce of bitterness. Her Bible was marked up. The cards she sent reflected her love and prayers over me. Her obedience unwavering and her demeanor grateful, she focused on the good things God had given her.

The day I found out what she lived through, I cried—not in sorrow, **but in awe.**

Surely, this was a woman who lived as more than a conqueror no matter what the enemy hurled her way. "The rain came down, the streams rose, and the winds blew and beat against that house; yet it did not fall, because it had its foundation on the rock" (Matthew 7:25, NIV).

If you know someone like that, then you know that kind of faith is *contagious*. Even though years have passed since my grandma went to be with the Lord, her life has had a powerful domino effect as I face my own storms.

The opposite can happen too.

Forty-five years before Caleb inherited his Promised Land, he stood among a sea of doubters. While he was unwaveringly ready for his portion, most of the spies spread "a bad report about the land they had explored" (Numbers 13:32, NIV). *Millions of people* were influenced by these *ten fearful individuals*—and they faced a lifetime outside of the promise because of it.

Makes me wonder, who's influencing *us*? Which voices are *we* taking into serious consideration? Are they from God . . . or not?

I'm gonna shoot straight with you. The stakes are high, and your answer matters. If it didn't, those Israelites would've entered the Promised Land regardless. It's the difference between being stuck in the wilderness, always looking off to a land you desperately want but *voluntarily surrendered*—and stepping into the Promised Land, gulping down milk and honey, and resting in God's good plan.

Other voices will urge you to bow out in fear, but God's voice will *always* call you to rise up in faith. This is your time. Which pathway will you choose? Eyes are watching, and when you rise up, you challenge others to do the same.

TAKE THE NEXT STEP

Will you follow the majority, or will you, like Caleb, follow the Lord wholeheartedly (Joshua 14:8)?

It's never too late. The voice of fear you entertained yesterday can be submitted to God right now. Since "the land on which your feet have walked will be your inheritance and that of your children forever" (Joshua 14:9, NIV), how about we choose faith today.

IN YOUR POST-BATTLE ANALYSIS remember . . .

1. Make a list of trials + enemies defeated
2. Recognize the legacy your predecessors left
3. Mine the deeper meanings of your battles
4. Determine what needs delegating to set up those following in your footsteps
5. Drive out any remaining enemies that pull you away from God
6. Commit every misfortune to the God who takes curses + turns them into blessings
7. Live knowing your inheritance is secure + in Christ, nothing to lose
8. Trust that our good God intentionally planted you where you are so you can thrive in the Land of Promise!
9. Recognize every blessing as grace
10. Analyze the voices of influence in your life + align yourself with those from God

MILEPOST 8

Plotlines of Purpose

Think about the story God is writing in your life. What about the stories of your spouse, friends, and family? Your kids, neighbors, and coworkers?

Let's give this some thought. Since no two autobiographies are the same, *every single person would tell you a different story.* That's the cool thing about our creative God—He didn't copy and paste but delighted in crafting something unique for each of us.

But it goes even beyond that. The unique parts of your story are not crafted solely for your own benefit, but as a witness to others. If we would take the time to get to know one another, we'd discover each person is a living character witness for our Great God. Just like authors leave imprints of themselves within their books, the Author of our lives unearths more of who He is through our testimonies as well.

We'll find this to be true in the next ten days as we follow each tribe of Israel and explore their unique plot of inherited land. Every settlement will point us back to the Creator and Landlord of the land, and it all culminates as our fearless leader finally settles into his own digs.

The time has come for everyone to rest in their inheritance . . . **us, most certainly, included**.

71

Just as Strong as Yesterday

Joshua 14:10-15

Where does it seem like others haven't had to wait as long as you for answered prayer, healing, or help?

Among the sea of young Israelites waiting for their boundary lines to be surveyed, notice there were only two old men among *hundreds of thousands*, their white hair sticking out in the crowd. None of their peers—who were busted out of Egyptian slavery, witnessed the parting of the Red Sea, and wandered in the wilderness—were left to stand in this moment with Joshua and Caleb.

Yet here they were, decades later, looking at the very land they spied out forty-five years earlier. What must've felt ripped from their hands *back then*, we see now was merely reserved for *later*.

In this full-circle moment, we hear Caleb declare, "Here I am today, eighty-five years old! I am still as strong today as the day Moses sent me out; I'm just as vigorous to go out to battle now as I was then. Now give me this hill country that the LORD promised me that day" (Joshua 14:10-12, NIV).

While most his age would be ready for retirement, Caleb was ready to tackle the biggest challenge yet. Since he'd seen the area firsthand, this guy knew the hill country around Hebron would be no walk in the park. Not only were the people who scared off the prior generation still there, but it was near the Dead Sea, which was 1,300 feet below sea level—and Hebron was 2,800 feet *above* sea level. Just the climb to *reach* the city would be difficult,[1] and who knows what enemies they'd confront.

Yet Caleb was ready to scale the mountain and seize God's promises.[2] Other tribes didn't have to wait as long as he did, but that didn't diminish his blessing. Instead, he led the charge with full trust in God's timing.

The same can be said about us. No matter how long we've waited compared to others, we don't have to be "lacking in zeal." Instead, we can keep our "spiritual fervor, serving the Lord" (Romans 12:11, NIV). Just as vigorous, just as strong, the righteous who plant themselves in God's Word will find "their leaves never wither, and they prosper in all they do" (Psalm 1:3).

But take note: The metaphorical giants in our land will also stay as long as we let them. May today be the day we evict them, for the Lord Himself promised, "My servant Caleb has *a different attitude* than the others have. He has remained loyal to me, so I will bring him into the land he explored. His descendants will possess their full share" (Numbers 14:24, italics added).

The land is all yours, but is your attitude all in? Let's follow Caleb's footsteps as we face our own hill country, knowing God rewards obedience when the time is right.

TAKE THE NEXT STEP

How would you describe your attitude lately? Would you say it's different from nonbelievers? Even different from faithless believers?

God takes notice of your steadfast loyalty, so climb that mountain in confidence. Your reward is coming.

72

He's in the (Boring) Details

Joshua 15:1-12

Do you love a good map too?

It doesn't matter if we're just driving fifteen minutes to Grandma's. I'll still punch in her address, check traffic, and see if I can shave off a minute or two from the arrival time. *Casual Sunday drive? I know no such thing.*

Well before Siri's voice-activated navigation and even long before Joshua's expedition map, Jacob sketched out a road map for his sons in his end-of-life blessing (Genesis 49:1-28). For Judah, he covered the physical and the spiritual markers.

Not only will the wine in Judah's land be so plentiful that he could wash his clothes in a tub of it and not even Tide's bleach detergent could get it clean (Genesis 49:11)—proven when the original spies brought back a cluster of grapes "so large that it took two of them to carry it" (Numbers 13:23). But Judah's "hand will be on the neck of your enemies" (Genesis 49:8, NIV), and while his tribe was unmistakably hedged in by the Moabites, Philistines, Amalekites, and Edomites, they would soon be the lion leading the charge with authority over all Israel. Certainly, this was "all your relatives will bow before you" coming to pass (Genesis 49:8).

But the feather in Judah's cap was the promise that "the scepter will not depart from Judah . . . until the coming of the one to whom it belongs, the one whom all nations will honor" (Genesis 49:10). It would take about 1,600 years ***(!)*** to see this final prophecy play out.

> From David until the Herods, a prince of Judah was head over Israel. . . . Even under their foreign masters . . . Israel had a limited right to self-rule, until AD 7 . . . [when it] was taken away. . . . Rabbis considered it a disaster of unfulfilled Scripture. . . . Yet God's word had not been broken. Certainly, Jesus was alive then. Perhaps this was the very year He was 12 years old and discussed God's Word in the temple.[3]

Jesus Christ was the prophesied Messiah, from the tribe of Judah, born in Bethlehem, and later called the Lion of the tribe of Judah who has triumphed (Revelation 5:5).

Do you see? Judah's portion was not random or inconsequential. Through a boring chapter of detailed boundaries—"from the hilltop the boundary headed toward the spring of the waters of Nephtoah, came out at the towns of Mount Ephron and went down toward Baalah" (Joshua 15:9, NIV)—we see that God took *all of the above* into account. He was mapping out not just property lines, but a grand plan for the whole world, which His Son would be sent to fulfill in this exact territory.

The same is true for you. When you trust His road map—**no matter if you're on the longest route and unable to trim minutes**—you will find His plan unfolding in a way that's just as good and redemptive.

God still holds the world in His hands—and thankfully, He holds your life too.

TAKE THE NEXT STEP

How does it encourage you to know God is caring for the details?

No matter how boring the details of your life appear, know they still matter to God. He will work *all those things* together for good. He has it all mapped out.

73

The Real GOAT Father

Joshua 15:16-63

What's your dad like?

Is he attentive and loving, or angry and withdrawn? Do you have fond memories with him, or does your history cause you to wince?

On the one hand, we've seen Caleb as a valiant warrior and a faithful follower of God. But can you picture him as a loving father as well?

Proof #1: As he's driving out Anakites, Caleb offers, "I will give my daughter Aksah in marriage to the man who attacks and captures Kiriath Sepher" (Joshua 15:16, NIV). Not only was this customary in the Middle East, but Caleb knew how much fight still lay ahead. He wanted to make sure his daughter was protected and cared for by a brave soldier.

Proof #2: Once Caleb ensured Aksah and Othniel were settled in newlywed bliss, his daughter came back with quite the request: "You have already given me land in the Negev; now please give me springs of water, too" (Joshua 15:19).

Listen. Much of the Negev is desert—its name means "parched and dry."[4] I may have a black thumb, but I know water is essential to growing crops . . . which is kind of important to people living off the land like the Israelites.

But hold up, *springs* of water? In an area with few water sources, we're talking a valuable commodity. "Wherever a spring existed, it was likely to be the nucleus of a village”[5]—as in, this girl isn’t just requesting a drinking fountain to fill her Stanley. She’s requesting the moon—to be at the heart of the community and in charge of the welfare of their clan.

Caleb didn’t skip a beat. He “gave her the upper *and* lower springs” (Joshua 15:19, italics added).

Here’s where this comes full circle for us: “Wherever springs flowed, people considered the water to be ‘living.’”[6] What a coincidence since you, too, have a Father who lavishly gave you Living Water through His Son. And now “whoever believes in [Him] . . . rivers of living water will flow from within them” (John 7:38, NIV). As in, *you’re* now the hub, the light of the world, the city on a hill meant to bring life to those around you.

Make no mistake. Even better than Caleb, your heavenly Father is the best Dad you could ask for. He’s scandalously generous, full of compassion, forever looking out for you, and offering everything without hesitation.

So “come all you weary, come all you thirsty, come to the well that never runs dry. Drink of the water. Come and thirst no more. . . . Taste of His goodness. Find what you’re looking for.”[7]

TAKE THE NEXT STEP

How does your earthly father compare or contrast to your heavenly Father?

Like with Caleb, everything good is meant to point you to your true Parent, for God is everything lovely and nothing horrible. Let’s give Him the praise He deserves today.

74

It's Gonna Be Good Today + Beyond

Joshua 16:1–17:13

Ever jumped to conclusions?

You seem more rational than me, but if Ty is late and doesn't answer his phone, my mind immediately pictures a car accident and EMT resuscitation. Unable to imagine any other reasonable explanation, I call back-to-back-to-back until he texts, "Phone was on silent—just picking up groceries!"

About three hundred years before the Israelites entered the Promised Land, a boy was sold into slavery by his own brothers. Stripped of his home, his loving dad, and his comfortable future, Joseph spent each moment at the mercy of his owner. Even worse, a false accusation of rape snowballed into handcuffs and a prison sentence.

The trajectory of Joseph's life took a downward trend—*down* into the pit, *down* in his station of life, *down* into prison.[8] Maybe the direction of *your* life is going south too.

You had faith; your symptoms didn't get better.

You worked with integrity; someone else got the credit.

You offered God what you had; He didn't multiply it.

But one thing I've learned: It's dangerous to jump to conclusions before we know the whole story—in Joseph's life *and* in ours.

In just one day, Joseph was pulled out of prison and designated second-in-command over all Egypt, showing each downhill move was a stepping stone to now raise him up. Even then, it wasn't until he lived through famine, a reunion with his family, and his dad's death that Joseph was finally able to look back and realize, *My brothers didn't sell me . . . God sent me.*[9] He told them straight up, "You intended to harm me, but God intended it all for good. He brought me to this position so I could save the lives of many people" (Genesis 50:20).

We may not see it today. But *someday*, the faithful will be able to trace God's hand throughout their lives. He's preparing you now for what He's prepared *for* you ahead. Like Joseph, we just gotta hang on.

Wanna know another fun layer? God flipped every bad thing for good in Joseph's lifetime, but He didn't stop there. Centuries later, we witness "the allotment for the descendants of Joseph extended from the Jordan River near Jericho, east of the springs of Jericho, through the wilderness and into the hill country of Bethel" (Joshua 16:1).

Even when all Joseph hoped for was escape in his day, God had something grander in mind—generations of believers, a portion of the Promised Land, and a robust inheritance continuing to be unveiled. God was blessing Joseph well past the grave.

He is up to something just as wonderful in your family too. No matter if all hope seems lost, you can still trust Him: "Your faithfulness continues through all generations, as enduring as the earth you created" (Psalm 119:90, BSB).

TAKE THE NEXT STEP

Instead of being fixated on the details of your day, how can you trust God with the bigger picture?

Rest, knowing He's looking after you, your family, and your legacy with the long game in mind.

75

What You Have Is Already Enough

Joshua 17:14-18

The struggle against wanting MORE is real, **is it not?**

It starts young too. I give my daughter a cracker, and immediately she's holding out her other hand, "More?" I read a chapter to my kids before bed only to hear a chorus of "NO! ONE MORE!"

I can't blame it only on the kids though—I have a whole *shelf* of jeans, but after I (repeatedly) pined for my SIL's, she finally just bought me the same pair. And with three girls currently stuffed in a small bedroom and their brother cramped in a den the size of my closet, I'm battling the desire for more space on the daily.

I don't know where this desire for *more* rears its ugly head for you, but it was a problem in ancient Israel too.

We just witnessed the tribes of Joseph receiving the second land inheritance, but Ephraim and Manasseh talk back like a couple of teenagers. "Why have you given us only one allotment . . . ? We are a numerous people, and the Lord has blessed us abundantly" (Joshua 17:14, NIV).

Wait a second. Not only is their combined territory significant—second only to Judah with its 76,500 fighting men—but their combined population of 58,850 isn't much larger than their brother tribes either (spoiler: *who get much smaller territories*).

So . . . what gives?

Joshua pushes back with a little dry humor that makes me respect the man all the more: "If you are so *numerous* . . . and if the hill country of Ephraim is *too small for you* . . . go up into the forest and clear land for yourselves" (Joshua 17:15, NIV, italics added).

As in, they had more land. They just weren't living in it.

If we define covetousness as "wanting more of what you already have enough of,"[10] the two tribes of Joseph didn't need more—they just needed to do more with what they had.

They still weren't ready to concede: "The Canaanites who live in the plain have chariots fitted with iron" (Joshua 17:16, NIV).

Hold up though. God had said, "When you . . . face horses and chariots and an army greater than your own, do not be afraid. The LORD your God . . . is with you!" (Deuteronomy 20:1). God already assured victory *in these precise circumstances*, which makes me wonder. What victory has the Lord promised *us*, but we're too focused on the chariots instead?

Hear Joshua's words anew: "You will have not only one allotment but the forested hill country as well. Clear it, and its farthest limits will be yours; though the Canaanites have chariots fitted with iron and though they are strong, you can drive them out" (Joshua 17:17-18, NIV).

You, too, have all that you need despite what you're up against. In Christ, you are strong enough to drive out the darkness that remains. Timber! It's time to do more with what you've already been given.

But we gotta pick up our axe and go all in. ***You up for it?***

TAKE THE NEXT STEP

What are you fearing as something too great to overcome?

God has already told you He dwells within you, and He is greatest and strongest. With Him at your side, clear out and gain the land that's rightfully yours.

76

Don't Accept Less When God Has More

Joshua 18:1-3

What have you been putting off?

I can't be the only one with a stack of mail on the counter or a pile of laundry on what ***might be*** a chair. Or maybe it's a conversation you know you need to have or a shift in priorities you've felt the need to make.

Whether serious or trivial, you've been dragging your feet. Because it's easier to avoid. Even the thought is draining. You're scared to make the change.

I hear ya—and you know who else does? The seven other tribes of Israel. They could've raised their hand at any time like Caleb, Manasseh, and Ephraim to ask, "What about me? What about *our* land?"

But they didn't. In place of eagerness, we see apathy. Rather than bold faith, we witness indifference. Instead of moving out to claim their own homes, these Israelites were okay with settling in the land of Ephraim, bumming off their brothers as freeloaders and mere tent dwellers.

On the one hand, these guys have been through a lot. I'm exhausted after our family's four-hour road trip each fall—**and that's with a hot**

shower and springy mattress awaiting. Yet these families are coming off seven years of hauling their every belonging and fighting giants *at the same time*. So we can imagine the many reasons to hang back:

Fatigue. They were tired of going, going, going, and the remaining territories still lay a distance ahead.
Fear. This wasn't their first rodeo. They'd seen the giants, they'd fought the battles, and they knew any future ones could be just as threatening and daunting.
FOMO. At the moment, they were kickin' back in their neighbor's hot tub. But if they left, they would be on their own and have to say goodbye to friends.
Passivity. Waiting for God's promises to fall into your lap is easier than actively picking up arms to gain them.

But our guy Joshua tells it like it is. He straight-up asks, "How long are you going to wait before taking possession of the remaining land?" (Joshua 18:3).

Are we, too, putting off something God has called us to do? Are we riding on the coattails of someone else's relationship with God? Are we settling for less? It's easy to wave off the task of conviction until tomorrow. Or someday down the road when it's more convenient.

But as Joshua pushes the tribes out of the nest, maybe today is the day we stop accepting less than God has for us too. We've lived off the faith of others, but it's time to make it ours. We've kept quiet, but it's high time we spoke up. And we've walked past that laundry pile one too many times—this is the big day to put it away and sit in that chair. ***(Uff da, what got into me? Really got carried away with that last one!)***

Whatever it may be, let's answer Joshua's question "How long?" with "*Right now.*"

TAKE THE NEXT STEP

What are you settling for today?

C. S. Lewis said, “We are . . . like an ignorant child who wants to go on making mud pies in a slum because he cannot imagine what is meant by the offer of a holiday at the sea. We are far too easily pleased.” Instead of settling for mud pies, let’s seek out our full inheritance in Christ.

77

In Your Hands or His?

Joshua 18:4-10

Where are you fighting for control today?

After the chosen men take Joshua's recommendation and explore the unclaimed territory, they (**somehow**) agree on seven divisions. Hey, I struggle with balancing the Christmas present scale among our four kids, so I cannot imagine gauging soil quality, tracking level and mountainous regions, drawing lines around every city, ETC., to then present fair territories *so not a single person feels slighted.*

Yet they did it—**deserving nothing less than a standing ovation, IMO.**

But even then, decisions weren't final. God told Moses back in Numbers 26:55, "Be sure that the land is distributed by lot" (NIV).

With lot in no way equaling luck, these Israelites knew their fate wouldn't lie in the hands of chance. Rather, "the lot is cast into the lap, but its every decision is from the LORD" (Proverbs 16:33, NIV). The New Living Translation puts it this way: "We may throw the dice, but the LORD determines how they fall." **(Dare you to try out that verse on your kid next time you win family game night.)** They would wait on God to give the final say.

But what about us? "He's Got the Whole World in His Hands" isn't just a catchy children's song (**that'll remain stuck in your head hours upon hours**), but it's absolute truth: "In His hand is the life of every living thing and the breath of all mankind" (Job 12:10, ESV).

If you know His hand—recognize His inviting open palms, appreciate His protective grip, and expect His generous gestures—that's reassuring. Before you even see the lot you're assigned, you embrace it because you know He gives you not just what you need, but much more than you could ever ask or imagine.

Even so, we see we must do our part too. These men took *months* giving this project their all and then presented it as an offering to God—trusting Him to take it from there.

Can we do the same?

I love control as much as the next person, but I cannot heal every disease. I cannot restore every heartache. I do not have all wisdom to know all things. I am a limited human who can only do some things. But the good news is I have a great God who can do all things. I know the Giver of Wisdom who gives it generously to all without finding fault. And I know the One who "forgives all your sins and heals all your diseases, who redeems your life from the pit and crowns you with love and compassion, who satisfies your desires with good things" (Psalm 103:3-5, NIV).

Let's follow the way of these Israelites—doing what we can, giving our work to God as our best offering, and then trusting Him with the outcome. Knowing He has our best interests in mind, let's echo the psalmist: "In you, LORD my God, I put my trust. I trust in you; do not let me be put to shame" (Psalm 25:1-2, NIV).

TAKE THE NEXT STEP

How can you do your best in the assignment you've been given today?

Unclench your grip from it, surrendering the outcome to His trustworthy hands.

78

Mining Nuggets of Wisdom

Joshua 18:11–19:23

Bible pop quiz: Can you name all twelve tribes of Israel? Maybe like me, you can rattle off Judah and Benjamin like NBD . . . but what about Zebulun, Issachar, and Naphtali? **(I'm clenching my teeth, avoiding eye contact, so no judgment here.)**

Whether the tribes are familiar or not, let's mine out those important nuggets of wisdom with every lot drawn:

> ***Benjamin.*** As the smallest tribe, yet not chosen last, their placement in the order is noteworthy. God sees the small fry, the runt of the litter, and doesn't underestimate them. Rather, He cares for us all, setting our place in history too, no matter our station.
>
> The Benjamites also show us we can't equate size with capability and strength. Following Jacob's prophecy in Genesis 49, this tiny tribe would be known for having warriors like ravenous wolves; producing the first king, Saul; and controlling the major cities of Jerusalem, Jericho, and Bethel. **Tiny, *but mighty*.**
>
> (P.S. The mom in me delights in seeing Benjamin placed right next to big bro Joseph. As if they'd spent enough time apart in Genesis,

it seems just like our heavenly Father to restore their unity for all of time, does it not?)

Simeon. After both Levi and Simeon used their weapons for evil, Jacob's last words still echo, "Cursed be their anger, so fierce, and their fury, so cruel! I will scatter them in Jacob and disperse them in Israel" (Genesis 49:7, NIV).

Lo and behold, just like Levi was spread throughout Canaan, the tribe of Simeon found itself smack-dab in the middle of Judah, scattered among their cities. They were "the only tribe to receive an allotment within another tribe's inheritance."[11]

What I love: Just like Judah handed over some of his inheritance to benefit the undeserving Simeon, Jesus, from the tribe of Judah, gave His inheritance to sinners. Judah generously agreed to this plan without opposition.[12] It was Judah's choice, and it was Jesus' choice—both gave freely. What a generous God we serve!

Zebulun and Issachar. Once again, their founding father's prophecy proved true. He said, "Zebulun will live by the seashore and become a haven for ships" (Genesis 49:13, NIV), and after receiving the territory between the Mediterranean and the Sea of Galilee, they were known for their "seafaring, shipping, and trade."[13]

Interestingly enough, when Moses later blessed Zebulun, it was in the same breath with Issachar, as if they were meant to work together to "feast on the abundance of the seas, on the treasures hidden in the sand" (Deuteronomy 33:19, NIV).

Will we do the same as the body of believers? "He makes the whole body fit together perfectly. As each part does its own special work, it helps the other parts grow, so that the whole body is healthy and growing and full of love" (Ephesians 4:16). God never intended for us to do life alone but in tandem with our brothers and sisters in Christ. Together, may we feast on His abundance, on the hidden treasure of the Kingdom of Heaven (Matthew 13:44-46).

Look at you now! ***You're totally gonna sweep Bible trivia next round.***

TAKE THE NEXT STEP

Which of the lessons learned from these four tribes stands out most to you?

Take a step forward in these truths today and claim more of the Promised Land God has for you.

79

The Best for Last

Joshua 19:24

Where are you tempted to scramble and take the best for yourself? From grabbing the best donut at church to elbowing my way to closer seats at a concert, lemme just say **I'VE BEEN THERE**.

As the lots were drawn for the other tribes, we see Joshua waiting all the while. He's put every other person first, and we can bet this has *not* escaped God's notice. But before we get to Joshua, here are the final nuggets of wisdom to glean from the other tribes:

> *Asher*. This guy was born out of a jealous rivalry between sisters. Fast-forward to Genesis 49:20, and Jacob leaves him only a blessing: "Asher's food will be rich; he will provide delicacies fit for a king" (NIV). Moses later said, "Most blessed of sons is Asher; let him be favored by his brothers, and let him bathe his feet in oil" (Deuteronomy 33:24, NIV).
>
> This tribe did indeed receive fertile grounds abundant in oil trees.[14] But more significantly, we see that no matter the dysfunction and sin we're born into, God "is able to bless you abundantly, so that in all things at all times, having all that you need, you will abound in every good work" (2 Corinthians 9:8, NIV).

Naphtali. Given the best farmlands, this tribe was blessed to be a blessing.[15] We, too, are "enriched in every way to be generous in every way" (2 Corinthians 9:11, ESV). More than half of the world's people live on less than $2 a day, and if you make about $50,000 per year, you earn more than 99 percent of the population.[16] **Like Naphtali, let's use our blessings to bless someone else.**

Dan. This tribe was given the westernmost side of the Promised Land, but this isn't where they ended up. Having "trouble taking possession of their land," the Danites looked to the territory of Naphtali and attacked the town of Laish instead (Joshua 19:47). Now in the northernmost city, they're a *long way* from their inheritance—where idol worship and a fake priest telling them what they want to hear soon follow.[17]

Truth be told: We don't have to make our own way into the Promised Land when our God has freely given the Way. Before our desires drag us from life to death (James 1:14), let's return to the Lord, and He will put new desires in our hearts (Psalm 37:4).

Finally . . . Joshua. No one would've batted an eye if the leader claimed his land first. Instead, our hero takes what's left over. Far from feeling entitled, he is just happy to be in the Promised Land. **Do we have the same attitude?**

The cherry on top: Joshua ended up with the city Timnath-serah. Meaning "an abundant portion," this was actually the town he most wanted (Joshua 19:50). A more recent explorer said, "Of all the sites I have seen, none is so striking as that of Joshua's home, surrounded as it is with deep valleys and wild rugged hills."[18] When you take care of others, *man*, the Lord will take care of you.

The two aging, faithful spies are now dwelling in the land, bookending the distribution. **CUE THE HAPPY TEARS, *AMIRIGHT?*** Be assured today you won't be left with scraps either. Like with Joshua and Caleb, your faithful waiting will result in God's best for you.

TAKE THE NEXT STEP

Which lesson from these remaining tribes speaks to you today?

Consider ways you can move forward in these truths. *All in*, because it's *all yours*.

80

Before You Jump to Conclusions

Joshua 22:1-34

Who are your ride-or-dies? I'm talking about those people who have stood by you through thick and thin and have your back *no matter what.*

I've never told this story before, and I told my husband to keep this secret to his dying day, but now eighty days into this devotional together, I feel as if I can tell you anything? **So here we go.**

While I was in labor with my middle daughter, the contractions were coming so fast and furious that I could not deal. After shouting, "I WILL NOT PUSH UNTIL I GET AN EPIDURAL" (**ironic, I know, coming from a graduate of the all-natural Bradley Method**), I bit down on my husband's arm like a feral animal.

I wish I was kidding. I'm no better than the rabid raccoon in *Elf*, and I'm surprised Ty doesn't have the scar to prove it.

Can I tell you something though? He stuck by me (plus, had two more kids with me). Man, if that isn't a ride-or-die, **I don't know what is.**

After claiming the Promised Land, Joshua calls "together the tribes of Reuben, Gad, and the half-tribe of Manasseh" (Joshua 22:1). These guys stuck around until every territory had been claimed, and Joshua claps them on the back, saying, "You did it. You didn't desert your fellow tribes. Well done." After missing seven years of special days with their own families,[19] these ride-or-dies finally get to go home.

But on the way back, they erected an imposing altar, and "the whole community of Israel . . . prepared to go to war against them" (Joshua 22:12). But first, they sent leaders to ask, "How could you turn away from the LORD and build an altar for yourselves in rebellion against him?" (verse 16).

The three tribes cried out, "The LORD, the Mighty One, is God! He knows the truth, and may Israel know it, too! We have not built the altar in treacherous rebellion. . . . We fear that in the future your descendants will say to ours . . . 'The LORD has placed the Jordan River as a barrier. . . . You have no claim to the LORD'" (Joshua 22:22, 24-25).

It wasn't an altar to worship—just a monument to remind. By this simple conversation, "all the Israelites were satisfied and praised God and spoke no more of war" (Joshua 22:33).

In our world of social media and cancel culture, it seems people have no problem blasting strangers, even churches and pastors, online. But that should not be. Jesus says, "If another believer sins against you, go privately and point out the offense. If the other person listens and confesses it, you've won that person back" (Matthew 18:15).

But if you're unsuccessful . . . *rant about it online! Record a podcast about it! Share it in stories!* **Nope, it says bring a few others along and try again.** "If the person still refuses to listen, take your case to the church" (Matthew 18:16-17).

Too many don't even attempt to reach out to those they believe are straying before declaring war. But it's worth it to follow these leaders' example and actually *go to them* to talk it out, wanting above all else to "restore that person gently" (Galatians 6:1, NIV).

Who knows? We might be wrong in our assumptions, and like the western tribes, *they* might surprise *us*.

TAKE THE NEXT STEP

What judgments have you made about others lately?

Consider whether you need to talk privately with them. May the goal be not simply to be right but to "help that person back onto the right path" (Galatians 6:1).

WHEN DETERMINING YOUR PLOTLINES, don't forget . . .

1. Scale the mountainous challenges with a different attitude than nonbelievers
2. Trust God is in the details since He mapped out your life long ago
3. Drink from the Well of Living Water that will never go dry
4. God will bless you even well past the grave
5. Do more with what you've already been given

6. Refuse to settle for less than what God has for you
7. Do your best + present it to God, trust Him with the rest
8. Care for others + the Lord will take care of you
9. Mine the nuggets of wisdom to be found in both well-known + unfamiliar parts of Scripture
10. Honor others with gentleness, kindness + love

MILEPOST 9

Gather Around for Some Fatherly Advice

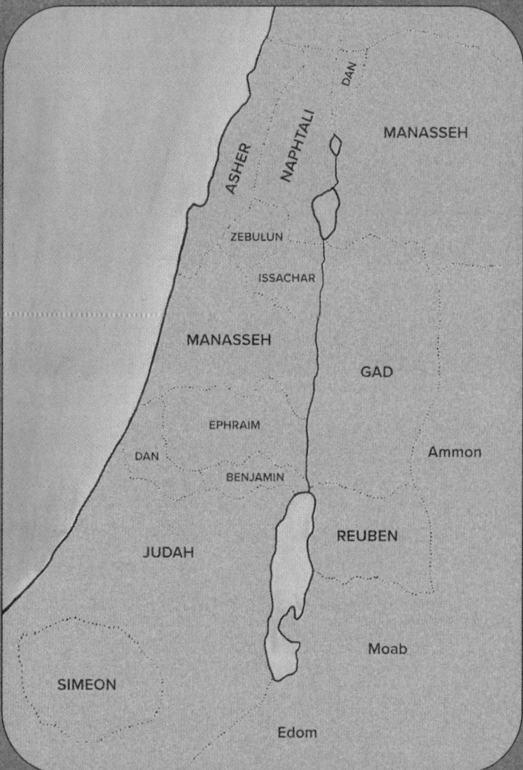

Have you ever heard someone's final words before they died? Maybe they reflected on their life, sharing regrets or highlights. Possibly they squeezed your hand and made known, "I love you." Or maybe they imparted words of wisdom you still hold dear.

This is Joshua. He's been warned by God Himself that his time is coming to a close, and these next ten days, we're going to lean in as our main man gives his final speech. We'll hear what he so *intently and intentionally* chose as his dying words.

Warning: Some of what he says may sound repetitive, and that's partly the point. Joshua looks back on the road he's traveled, and in a jam-packed chapter, he gives a summary of the most important lessons he's gleaned, words of encouragement he's clung to, and warnings he knows God's people continually need to hear.

Joshua's words were not just for the Israelites of his day but for even us today to heed as we seek to dwell in the Land of Promise ourselves.

So gather around in this final hour, and let's soak up every last drop of wisdom in this fatherly advice. Because Joshua delivers, he gives us the goods, with each sentence being important, and as you'll see, each thought significant.

81

He Was Faithful Then, He'll Be Faithful Now

Joshua 23:1-3

Who is that fatherly figure in your life?

You know, that wise person you look up to, who's lived a little more life than you have, whose opinion you respect and seek after? Could be your pastor, neighbor, or uncle. Could be your big brother, teacher, or boss.

Or like for me (and unlike the Israelites), **this could be your actual dad.**

Since the stipulation for entering Canaan was to wait until their parents died first, these sons and daughters all entered essentially as orphans. Who was left to teach them how to manage their 401(k) or change the oil? Who did they turn to for learning to tie a tie, set their fishing hook, grill the perfect steak, and well, *all practical help and life lessons*?

Mentors were slim pickings, but as one of only two men from the older generation allowed insider access to the Promised Land—not to mention being their actual chosen leader—Joshua would've been a top choice. So imagine the magnitude of this hour, as Joshua faces the final curtain. He calls together "all the elders, leaders, judges, and officers of Israel" for his parting words (Joshua 23:2), and they're all leaning in, waiting with bated breath.

Since he is a "type," or figure, of Christ, let's shoulder our way into the circle and soak up his wisdom too: "I am now a very old man. You have seen *everything the LORD your God has done for you during my lifetime.*" (Joshua 23:2-3, italics added).

Here's the CliffsNotes version of "*everything the Lord had done*":

- freed the Israelites out of slavery
- crushed the Egyptian army
- parted the Red Sea (and later, the Jordan River)
- led with a cloud by day, fire at night
- made water gush out of a rock
- rained food literally from the sky
- conquered every enemy of Canaan
- gave them rest in their Promised Land

Running parallel, we as God's people should reflect on everything Jesus has done and is doing for us:

- freed us from the bondage of sin and death (Romans 8:2)
- crushed the spiritual authorities by His victory on the cross (Colossians 2:15)
- shows us how to walk in new life when we come out of the waters of baptism (Romans 6:3-4)
- leads us night and day by the Spirit (Romans 8:14)
- is the Rock that offers Living Water (1 Corinthians 10:4)
- is the Bread of Life, "the true bread from heaven" (John 6:32)
- has already overcome (John 16:33)
- gives us Sabbath rest and leads us to our heavenly home, with no more tears or suffering (Hebrews 4:9-11; Revelation 21:4)

Like the Israelites, you have seen all the Lord has done "for your sake." He has fought your enemies and brought you this far for your *benefit.*

Surely, He won't abandon you or drop the ball *now*. Unquestionably, the Lord your God has good for you and will be faithful throughout your lifetime. Let's not wait until our dying breath to reflect. No, you and me, let's stop and give thanks *now*.

TAKE THE NEXT STEP

Which of these truths about Jesus will you dwell on today?

Take the time to consider all the Lord has done for you, and thank Him.

82

This Land Is Yours, Not Theirs

Joshua 23:4-5

Do you know someone who's faced a battle similar to yours?

Maybe you both went through a divorce or struggled against anxiety. Or possibly you each lost a job, a parent, or your health. Or you were both raised in abusive homes, dysfunctional families, or legalistic religions that never taught about a relationship with Jesus.

I gotta know—did you respond identically? Or did you choose different reactions . . . and thus different paths and conclusions?

Not long ago, I was sitting on white, crinkly paper, recounting to my doctor the oncologist's warning of how I run the biggest risk for secondary cancer these next five years. "I still battle fear more than I'd like," I said. "But I'm also still convinced of the goodness of God."

I'll never forget her reply: "I've seen a lot of cancer patients—and they either walk out of it focused on the positive or they wind up bitter."

AS IF SHE DIDN'T READ MY FIRST BOOK where I echo this very thought: "Interesting how we can walk along the same paths as others yet come to very different conclusions, isn't it? . . . One person goes through infertility, chemotherapy, or a furlough at work with total fear and signs off in defeat. Another? Strangely hopeful, somehow filled with peace. . . . [We] don't need to have a story shaded by anger or darkened by bitterness. . . . that was what others chose, but P.S. *We don't have to.*"[1]

Joshua says, "Remember how I have allotted as an inheritance for your tribes all the land of the nations that remain. . . . The Lord your God himself will push them out for your sake . . . and you will take possession" (Joshua 23:4-5, NIV).

Look up the word "allotted" and you'll read "assigned or distributed as a portion, share, or lot."[2] The *Cambridge Dictionary*, **which, coming from the birthplace of the English language, would know best IMO**, describes it as "given or made available for a particular purpose."[3]

Here's the thing: The Lord assigned and gave them the land. He promised to push out any obstacle. The land overflowing with milk and honey was made available—to them, not their enemies. God had a divine purpose for them there. It was just on them to take possession.

In the same respect, we're given free, abundant life in Christ. He has overcome any barriers to claiming it. This land overflowing with peace, joy, love, and hope is rightfully ours—and it's already made available, like *right now*. We're all given this same invitation, but *will we seize it?* **Others may not, but what about you?**

It doesn't matter what form adversity takes—Anakites or cellulite, walls of Jericho or walls of metaphor, the sin of Achan or the sin of our old nature—it's not their land. Your inheritance in Christ has been allotted, and it's all *yours*. Will you take possession of it? All of heaven is hoping you say yes.

TAKE THE NEXT STEP

How can you move forward into land that has already been conquered for you by Jesus but remains unclaimed?

Step out in faith to possess and occupy your inheritance through the power of the Holy Spirit.

83

Be Careful

Joshua 23:6-8, 11

Who or what influences you most? Culture's norms or your family's long-held traditions? Your closest friends or those colleagues you talk to on the daily? Your spouse or social media, where those you follow are literally called influencers?

I think about this constantly when it comes to my kids, knowing that "bad company corrupts good character" (1 Corinthians 15:33, NIV). Who they are exposed to and develop relationships with *matters*—and while I can't oust certain peers from their classrooms (**believe me, I've got names**), I do not let the cards fall as they may when it comes to their teachers.

Rather, I scour the trusted source that is Facebook (**kidding**) and analyze each candidate in a way I feel the CIA would be proud of. Once I find Bible verses, Jesus fish, and cross necklaces on their pages, I submit a teacher request form (**partly kidding**).

Here's where this comes full circle for us: After Joshua reminds Israel of their God and their inheritance, he warns, "Be very careful to follow everything Moses wrote. . . . Make sure you do not associate with the other people still remaining in the land. Do not even mention the names of their gods. . . . Rather, cling tightly to the LORD your God as you have done until now. So be very careful to love the LORD your God" (Joshua 23:6-8, 11).

Do you see that phrase Joshua repeated *twice*? "Be very careful . . ."

As in, pay attention to who you're following. Be vigilant about what you do. And be watchful of potential dangers so you can avoid harm or mistakes.

Jesus gives this same warning to us:

- Do not be deceived by the empty words of partners of darkness, but walk as children of light (Ephesians 5:6-8).
- Flee from idolatry and don't participate with demons (1 Corinthians 10:20).
- Don't be conformed to this world but be transformed by the renewing of your mind (Romans 12:2).

How do we do all of that? Joshua was clear, just as the Word has been clear: **Obey and "cling tightly" to God.**

Guess what? This is the same phrase used in Genesis 2:24 to describe the close relationship between husband and wife, so ultimately, obeying looks like *loving*. Be careful and give serious attention to "love the Lord your God with all your heart, all your soul, all your mind, and all your strength" (Mark 12:30).

The opposite of taking care is *neglect*. It's our choice: **What will we give our attention to and what will we ignore?** Let's heed the words of Jesus and Joshua and "cling tightly to the Lord your God as you have done until now" (Joshua 23:8), allowing Him to influence us instead of allowing others to sway us away from the Lord.

TAKE THE NEXT STEP

In what areas do you feel the Lord calling you to be extra careful?

The people around us influence us—for better or for worse, toward the Lord or away. What relationships do you need to give serious attention to? And who do you need to Facebook stalk? *(Okay, now I'm really kidding.)*

84

It's Already a Done Deal

Joshua 23:9-10

Are you waiting for victory, living in victory, or moving forward in victory?

Let's be real. As a mom, I know how important proper verb tense is: "I have to go to the bathroom," "I'm going to the bathroom," and "I went to the bathroom" are very different situations that compel very different reactions. One requires scooping up my kid like a football, sprinting straight to the toilet. The others have me veering off to the shower for a good ol' fashioned hose-down.

Verb tense is equally important with God's promises. Long ago in Deuteronomy, before the Israelites even set foot in the Promised Land, God reassured them, "See, I *have given* you this land. Go in and take possession of the land the LORD swore He would give to your fathers" (1:8, NIV, italics added).

Notice "*have given*." As in, it's a done deal, officialized in the *past*.

How could we be sure, though? When there were still Canaanites within the borders? When the battle hadn't even started?

Yet our God doesn't misspeak. He spoke of it as a past action for a reason—and not just this once. *Fourteen different times* God assured them, "I'll give you the land."[4] In His eyes, their victory was as good as done.

Fast-forward to 1 Corinthians 15:57, and Paul says, "Thanks be to God! He gives us the victory through our Lord Jesus Christ" (NIV). In what verb tense do we receive this promise?

Present tense.

Which means we don't need to live off past victories as if we've spent all there is and have nothing more to hope for. Nor do we have to wait around for some future victory to solidify our standing.

Because of Jesus' triumph over sickness, demons, nature, and death, it is finished. Our salvation is accomplished, and our victory is sure.

This is what Joshua wanted God's people to know before he walked the streets of gold. Encompassing all tenses, the victory—past, present, and future—wouldn't happen through the Israelites' own strength. Rather, it was the LORD who "has driven out before you great and powerful nations; to this day no one has been able to withstand you. One of you routs a thousand, because the LORD your God fights for you, just as he promised" (Joshua 23:9-10, NIV).

God was the Source of their victory. *He* was the Reason, *He* holds all the power, and *He* will keep every last one of His promises.

The same is true for us. To answer my initial (**trick**) question **#sorry**, your triumph isn't relegated to just one tense. In Christ, you can wait expectantly for victory to come. In Christ, you can live in victory today. And in Christ, you can move forward from the past into already-given victory as well. *It's all of the above.* **You, my friend, get the whole kit and caboodle!**

Don't ever forget it: The God who's already overcome the trials of this world now asks you, more than a conqueror, to go out and fight the battle—because it's a done deal, the victory is already all yours, and the victory is coming.

TAKE THE NEXT STEP

Which tense of your victory is hardest to believe—past, present, or future?

Trust that God is fighting for you today and has already deemed you an overcomer.

85

Who or What Have You Made an Ally?

Joshua 23:12-13, 16

"Do you want to form an alliance with me?"

Please tell me you know who said that quote. I'll give a hint: season 1, episode 4. On the brink of their office downsizing, Dwight singles out Jim to join forces, mine information, and pool their connections to (hopefully) come out on top.

The Office memes aside, who would *you* team up with in hopes of solving your current dilemma, challenge, or trial? A doctor specializing in your condition? A coworker with similar convictions? Or a praying spouse or parent who will battle on their knees for your family?

In the middle of Joshua's famous last speech, he warns, "If you turn away and ally yourselves with the survivors of these nations . . . and if you intermarry with them and associate with them . . . the LORD your God will no longer drive out these nations before you. Instead, they will become snares and traps for you, whips on your backs and thorns in your eyes, until you perish from this good land" (Joshua 23:12-13, NIV).

If ever a thorn or splinter gets lodged in your eye, (1) **OW,** I thought a sliver underfoot was bad enough, and (2) eye specialists say in response to this very thing, "It is important to act quickly."

Not that you'd want to keep a splinter around, what with the sharp pain every time you blink, but the best course of action is quite simple:

Remove it ASAP. Otherwise, this splinter could either scratch your cornea (**which BTW helps you see and take in light**) or jump straight to infection.

Here's what I'm getting at with this random discourse on ocular health: If the Israelites allied themselves with the Canaanites, God would let them do it. He wouldn't force their allegiance. But foreknowing all, He warned of what would certainly come: Their godless neighbors would cause vision changes, obstructing their ability to see and limiting the power of their sight—ultimately resulting in blindness to their very God.

Again though, if dealt with quickly, the eye would rapidly heal since the cornea is one of the fastest healing tissues in the body.[5] Likewise, by swiftly driving out their enemies, the Israelites could save themselves a lot of trouble. They could bask in the Light, carry on free of pain, and maintain full range of vision.

In the same respect, something so small in *our* lives can cause so much pain. Let a little worry fester here, a bit of anger grow there, and it won't be long until it consumes us and leads to further destruction.

Let's heed this warning today though, avoid any out-of-pocket expense, and act quickly, refusing to make any alliance with this world, but only with the one true God.

TAKE THE NEXT STEP

Who or what will you form an alliance with today?

Hear Jesus whisper, "No one can serve two masters. For you will hate one and love the other" (Matthew 6:24). Let's "put to death the sinful, earthly things lurking within you" (Colossians 3:5) and choose Jesus.

86

The Cost Is Great, but the Price Is Greater

Joshua 23:14-15

Are you, too, a sucker for freebies?

No shame in my game. You can always spot me waving my arms to catch a free tee at sports games. We sign up for every free trial before paying for the real deal. And if I can load my diaper bag with free candy at a parade, well, scoot aside, children. M&M's are at stake, and **I'M STOCKING UP FOR THIS YEAR'S TRUNK OR TREAT**.

But my kids are an easier target. "This app is free!" *(Though it requires inside purchases.)* "I get free lunches!" *(As our tax dollars go up.)* "This game has a free trial!" *(Just need a credit card to charge when we forget to cancel seven days later.)*

There's a reason people say, "There's no such thing as a free lunch." Whether time, money, or personal information, there's always a price to pay or strings attached.

This is exactly what Joshua was calling out for the Israelites. He made sure they were well aware of the good stuff—their inheritance, the assurance that God Himself will drive out their enemies, and the promise of His faithfulness to the end.

Yet just as importantly, they needed to know there was a price to pay.

The way ahead would require them to work, battle giants, and be obedient to God—not to mention, "If you break the covenant of the Lord your God by worshiping and serving other gods, his anger will burn against you, and you will quickly vanish from the good land he has given you" (Joshua 23:16). **Uff da!**

It's important to realize it's the same for us. Jesus offers everything good, His love, and abundant life. We truly lack *nothing* in the benefits package of our inheritance in Christ.

Yet we must also know following Jesus looks like giving up our own way, taking up our cross, and surrendering our lives to Him. If that's not our thing and we turn the other way like the Israelites did, He'll give us what we want—removing His protective hand and leaving us to face the consequences . . .

But guess what? While the cost of following Christ is so high that it demands your very life, the cost of turning away? **Far greater.** Jesus assures us, "You will be repaid at the resurrection of the righteous" (Luke 14:14, NIV), and I love how John Piper interprets this: "There is no cost that you can pay in following Me that won't be made up to you a thousandfold in the resurrection."[6]

Truly, since Jesus paid it all, living life with Him is *only ever gain.*

TAKE THE NEXT STEP

What's the cost of obedience or disobedience in the choices you face today?

Let Joshua's words, as well as Jesus' promise, advise your next steps. His Word will never lead you astray!

Rehearse Your Roots

Joshua 24:1-13

Do you catch yourself retelling the same stories?

I used to think I wouldn't do this until I hit grandparent status. You know, like when my memory fades and I forget who I am, I'll rehash birth stories and random grocery store encounters to my kids no matter how many times I've already mentioned them.

But no. I'm a thirty-seven-year-old whippersnapper of a mom, and I retell stories *on purpose.*

"Oscar, remember how you used to carry around a ladle like a stuffed animal?" *Yes, Mom.*

"Mabel, did you know even when you were rocking on your bouncer as a baby, you and the cat were inseparable?" *Yep.*

"Hazel, have I told you why we call you our honey girl?" *Yeah, I think 1Mx and counting.*

"Dottie, can you believe we let the internet decide your name with a reel that went viral?" **True story.**

Joshua's the same. He gathers the tribes of Israel like library story time, and in a matter of thirteen verses, He packs five hundred years of history into one short story. Like a short tweet on X instead of a long-winded video on YouTube, Joshua retold the faithfulness of the Lord Almighty. From Abraham's father, Terah, back in Genesis 11, all the way down to the Israelites in the present day.

Yep, God was the One who led Abraham into the land all those years ago.

You bet He delivered their ancestors from Egyptian slavery.

He indeed was the One who drove out the Amorites.

Here's what's noteworthy: ***None of this was new news for anyone.*** No one's holding their breath over how this story's gonna end. They've heard it so many times, they could rehearse it in their sleep. But it was drilled into them because it was *important.*

We would do well to follow Joshua's example. Who are those under you? Those under your influence? Those in your circle? Like a mother hen gathering her chicks, summon those near and far. Invite them for brunch. Host a holiday. Spare a couple minutes before bed . . . and retell the stories of old.

Don't assume they know it all. Even if they can parrot it back, it doesn't matter. Tell them about Jesus—His saving grace and powerful authority. His unconditional love and all-surpassing peace. His wide-open arms and promise of heaven.

Studies show that retelling stories builds resiliency and kids face challenges better and learn to cope with trials in healthy ways. It also fosters belonging and identity, with "a deep knowing that we belong to something bigger than ourselves," and it soothes the pressures of this world and binds families together.[7]

This is just the findings for the *immediate* family—imagine what can happen in retelling the grander story of God within our *spiritual* family too. Repetition was key then, and no doubt about it, *it's key today too.*

TAKE THE NEXT STEP

Who can you gather today to retell the important stories?

Don't delay, and don't quit. Like a broken record, let's be the Joshuas of our day, retelling the goodness of God to anyone who will listen.

88

Bury It in a Burial

Joshua 24:14-16

Hypothetical question: If you were forced out of your house today and could only grab three things to take with you, what would they be?

I'm not gonna lie—I'd swipe the children, my laptop with its files of my life's work, and my espresso maker. **(Ty can walk out on his own two feet, no?)**

Back in Genesis 31, when a man named Jacob realized his in-laws were growing resentful toward him, he hightailed it out of town with his family, livestock, and possessions. However, what does his wife Rachel do on her way out? She "stole her father's household idols and took them with her" (Genesis 31:19).

Skip ahead to chapter 35 and Jacob tells "everyone in his household, 'Get rid of all your pagan idols, purify yourselves, and put on clean clothing. We are now going to Bethel, where I will build an altar to the God who answered my prayers when I was in distress. He has been with me wherever I have gone.' So they gave Jacob all their pagan idols and earrings, and he buried them under the great tree near Shechem" (Genesis 35:2-4).

No longer would they trust in anyone but God. Instead of placing too much importance on worldly things or looking to anything but God to guide them and fulfill their needs, Jacob made a vow to the Lord that He alone would be their God—and he meant to keep it.

But it took burying the idols to do so.

Fast-forward to Joshua's final words. As he stands in the same place—Shechem—centuries after Jacob, leading the people to renew their covenant with God, we hear a similar speech: "So fear the Lord and serve him wholeheartedly. Put away forever the idols your ancestors worshiped. . . . Serve the Lord alone" (Joshua 24:14).

We may not run the temptation of bowing to a golden calf or worshiping a wooden statue, but what idols might we be holding onto instead?

Wealth, success, security?

Health, food, our phones?

Comfort, approval, relationships?

John Piper says, "If we come to crave, love, depend upon, and trust for a blessing people's praise to enhance our self-exaltation . . . or [if we trust] money, or power, or sex, or family, or productivity, or anything else besides God Himself for the greatest blessing, help, guidance, and satisfaction, then . . . we are doing what idolatry has always done."[8]

Even if like Rachel, you held on to an idol yesterday, and even if like the Israelites, you once worshiped another god above the one true God, you can choose a new beginning today.

Remember: "Buried" involved a burial—meaning, we put it to death, for it is *already dead.* Putting aside things that neither see, hear, brew coffee, nor live, we can instead renew our covenant with our God who is very much alive, speaking to us, hearing us, leading us, protecting us, and redeeming us.

TAKE THE NEXT STEP

What are the idols you've taken with you along the road of life?

What do you say we remove them from our lives and bury them *once and for all.*

89

All Means All

Joshua 24:1-14

Do you love absolutes as much as my kids do?

One day, it's "Mom, you ALWAYS say no . . ."

The next it's "You NEVER let me . . ."

And sprinkled in between, it's "But EVERYBODY else gets to do that!"

I finally said, "I don't *always* say no, but I can certainly start now if you think that anyways—and we can see how that really feels?" **(I sound real fun, don't I?)** I laughed the next time Oscar wanted something. He came with palms up and asked diplomatically, "So since I know you don't *always* say no when I want a snack right before dinner, can I have a granola bar?"

Nice try. **(And between us, that answer is always no.)**

As Joshua continues his farewell speech and relays "what the LORD, the God of Israel, says" (Joshua 24:2, NIV), we see a different type of absolute. Don't miss all the things God repeatedly had done for His people:

I took (verse 3)
I led (verse 3)
I gave (verse 4)
I sent (verse 5)
I afflicted (verse 5)
I did (verse 5)
I brought (verse 6)
I put (verse 7)
I did (verse 7)
I brought (verse 8)
I gave (verse 8)
I destroyed (verse 8)
I delivered (verse 10)
I gave (verse 11)
I sent (verse 12)
I gave (verse 13)

He did it *all*, in a variety of actions and in a plethora of ways. Tracing God's hand from the beginning, we see that He made a pact with Abraham, bringing him into the land and promising that his descendants would dwell there too. Even when Jacob went down to Egypt, it didn't thwart God's purposes. As we've spent (*nearly!*) one hundred days watching Him bring His people back, we have more than enough evidence to determine God always keeps His word. Every prophecy was fulfilled.

"Deep in your hearts you know that every promise of the LORD your God has come true. Not a single one has failed!" (Joshua 23:14).

Because we have our own set of absolute promises God always keeps, we can say the same (italics added). Deep in my heart, I know . . .

> "With God *all things* are possible" (Matthew 19:26, NIV).
> "In *all things* God works for the good of those who love him" (Romans 8:28, NIV).
> "In *all things* at *all times,* having *all* that you need, you will abound in every good work" (2 Corinthians 9:8, NIV).
> "I can do *all things* through him who strengthens me" (Philippians 4:13, ESV).

It doesn't matter where we stand on the timeline of life—beginning, middle, or near the end—we can know, as surely as Joshua and the Israelites, that "He who began a good work in you will carry it on to completion" (Philippians 1:6, NIV).

What God says in His Word will certainly come to pass, and we, too, will find life in the Land of Promise.

TAKE THE NEXT STEP

Which of these promises stands out most to you today?

Like D. L. Moody said, "God never made a promise that was too good to be true." So let's wait expectantly for His promises to come to fruition.

90

As for Me and My House

Joshua 24:14-16

Wouldn't life be easier if you could control people?

Ha! Hear me out. I'm not out to be a tyrant or to be overbearing. I just mean, if I could force my kids to always flush the toilet, freely share instead of selfishly hoard, and stop the earsplitting habit of whining, I'd do it in a heartbeat.

And if you could make your in-laws speak to you respectfully or be attentive grandparents, you'd be up for it too, right? If you could force your boss to honor work-life balance or show some recognition now and then, would you even bat an eye? Or what about our neighbors—if we could get them to pick up their dog's tootsie rolls, or better yet, *take care of business in their own yard*, WOULD WE NOT?

Or maybe that last one's just me . . .

Anyways. The problem is we can't. As much as we'd like to force people to get in line when we know better, we realize that everyone makes their own decisions—no matter their age.

While we can't control others, though, we can control ourselves, "for God gave us a spirit not of fear but of power and love and self-control" (2 Timothy 1:7, ESV).

Joshua knew this full well. After he lays out everything God has done for His people throughout history, he declares, "Serve the LORD alone.

But if you refuse to serve the LORD, then choose today whom you will serve. . . . But as for me and my family, we will serve the LORD" (Joshua 24:14-15).

Joshua was wise not to force the issue. As much as he knew God was better and wished for those around him to realize it too, Joshua couldn't coerce them to love Him.

But he could choose for himself who he would serve, and he would lead his family to love the Lord with all their heart, soul, and mind as well.

I don't know if you're surrounded by believers or if those in your own home have strayed from the straight and narrow. But I do know that, no matter *their* choice, you can still make the decision for *yourself* to follow Him.

(But someday, they'll learn to flush, right?)

TAKE THE NEXT STEP

Who (or what) do you choose to serve today? How might your decision ripple out to those around you?

Ask the Lord for opportunities to share about Him with those you love. Who knows? Maybe today is the day they, too, declare, "As for me and my family, we will serve the Lord."

FINAL WORDS FOR God's people

1. Recall everything the Lord has done for you
2. Remember you've been allotted an inheritance in Christ + it's time to take possession of it
3. Be very careful to obey
4. Your victory is past, present + future
5. Make no alliance with the world but only with God
6. The cost of following God is high but only ends in gain
7. Retell stories about who your God is + what He's done
8. Bury your dead idols
9. Be confident every one of God's promises is true
10. Choose today whom you will serve + invite others to do the same

MILEPOST 10

Truths to Take with You into the Promised Land

I gotta be honest, when my publisher said, "Let's do a one-hundred-day devotional next!" **I blinked real hard**. Admittedly, as someone who's never made it through a thirty-day fitness or diet challenge, who dropped off the gratitude-journal wagon only a few days in, and who's never even tracked a streak on the read-your-Bible app, I wondered aloud, "Does anyone do *anything* that long?"

But guess what happened?

I made a chart with one hundred blank spots for one hundred days, and as I followed the footsteps of the Israelites through the Promised Land, I filled out key ideas along the way. By the time I finished mapping their progress, I looked down at exactly, precisely, *one hundred completed lines.*

I knew then that this was the journey God had for you and me to take together, and man, are we gonna finish strong.

These next ten days, we're going to wrap up final lessons from Joshua's life, fast-forward to the future to learn what steps the Israelites take next (**and which ones we would be wise to avoid**), and ultimately, look heavenward to a better country and our forever homeland.

I'm proud of (**and amazed by**) you for making it this far, and I trust the Lord still has more for you in the pages ahead.

You still in?

91

The Title Then vs. Now

Joshua 24:14-16

What are you known for? Or what names are you called?

Maybe like Ty, you're the baker of the family, famous for your sourdough pizza or Swedish pancakes. Maybe the green thumb, also well-known for your bouquets of blooming dahlias. You're celebrated for what you do, and it's well deserved. **Hats off to you!**

Or maybe like me, you're known for something you've battled or been through, and it's not exactly something you like reliving . . . Addict. Outcast. Control Freak. Perfectionist. Victim. Failure. Cynic.

Cancer Survivor.

Blah.

What about SAHM? Wife? Christian, author, speaker, social media influencer? I'll take any of those! I'd even prefer Overseer of the Laundry Pile or Owner of the House with Plastic Nativity Characters Constantly Strewn All over the Yard. **Yep, you got her—I'm right here!**

But I get it. On the one hand, it's true. I *was* diagnosed with cancer, and not only was it a monumental time in my life back *then*—it affects me presently, too, in more ways than I could've imagined.

Also, God used it for good in crazy ways. He showed up, cutting my treatment in half. He brought my husband into the picture when I was sharing my diagnosis at church. God used my blog about it to pivot my career from kids ministry to devotional and Bible study writing.

More than these external miracles, He did a work internally too. He met my tears in the nights alone with His comforting Word. He held my hand during hour-long scans, enveloping me in His peace. And through the care of His people, the declarations in worship songs, and the power of prayer, He convinced me once and for all that He will flip everything bad for good.

But must we boil down my whole identity to a disease I pray never returns? As if that's all I am, the most significant thing about me, the core of my entire being?

In the very first verse of the very first chapter of Joshua, our hero is described as "Joshua son of Nun, Moses' assistant." That's what he was known for. Like Assistant to the Regional Manager, junior started out as a lackey, an understudy, a subordinate.

Fast-forward to the last chapter, and we read, "Joshua son of Nun, the servant of the Lord, died at the age of 110" (Joshua 24:29).

Not "leader of God's people." Not "commanding officer of the Israelite army." And not "conqueror of the Promised Land" either. Rather, the title marking his tombstone was *servant.* He was still performing duties for another Leader, lower in status than his Superior.

And yet, this was the highest calling.

As God's people, let's be known for one thing: "Well done, my good and faithful servant" (Matthew 25:21). Instead of making a name for ourselves, let's live as if being God's servant is the highest calling . . . **because it is.**

TAKE THE NEXT STEP

What would it look like to live your life so you're known as a Servant of the Living God?

The Greek word for *servant* literally means "a slave or bondservant, someone who sets aside all rights of his own to serve another."[1] Let's take Joshua's cue and live as God's servants above all other titles.

92

We Don't Work for Victory—But from It

Joshua 24

Would you describe your current season as hard or easy, good or bad?

Not necessarily light reading, but if we were to pull up Joshua's obituary for funsies, we'd see he lived to the whopping age of 110.

Let's do the math. If he lived forty years in Egypt and another forty in the wilderness, that means he spent thirty years in the Promised Land. Since he spent seven of those years fighting the Canaanites, he lived only his last twenty-three years in his territorial allotment.

Here's what we need to realize: His forty years in Egypt were not easy. Under the wrath of slave drivers, he worked around the clock.

Then the next forty? Joshua was subjected to life in the wilderness, "not as a result of *his* disobedience, mind you, but because of the lack of faith that paralyzed the rest of God's people."[2]

Then, at eighty, Joshua finally gets to taste and see the Promised Land. Yet instead of pitching a tent, rolling out a welcome mat, and calling it good, he still had to battle for what was his. Year after year, he trudged on, sword in hand and his God by his side, until finally, he could kick back in retirement because "the Lord had given the people of Israel rest from all their enemies" (Joshua 23:1).

*In the tone of Bing Crosby, **Do you see what I see?***

Much of Joshua's life was working, battling, and seizing—and much of the Christian's life is the same.

Don't get me wrong. Life is FULL of joy. That first sip of coffee in the morning. Finishing a good book. The warm sun on your skin (well, all five minutes for us redheads before we're scorched with third-degree burns). Belly laughing with friends. Bear hugs from your kids. The feeling of home with your spouse.

But while we journey toward heaven, there will also be giants in the land. Walls blocking our path. Slave drivers attempting to put us back under the yoke. Disobedience that sets us back. Mountains to climb, valleys to navigate, and barren lands to fertilize.

It should all be expected. ***But an even greater reality is also ours.***

No matter the terrain, you have a promise from the living God: "I have been given all authority in heaven and on earth . . . and be sure of this: I am with you always, even to the end of the age" (Matthew 28:18, 20).

Like Joshua, you can persevere through Egypt, remain faithful in the wilderness, lead the charge into the Promised Land, overcome the enemy, and seize all God has for you—because "despite all these things, overwhelming victory is [yours] through Christ, who loved [you]" (Romans 8:37).

It may be a whole lot of work, but remember: We don't work *for* victory . . . we work *from* it. Like Joshua, remain faithful, and at the end of your life you won't regret it either. **Rest from your enemies is a'comin'.**

TAKE THE NEXT STEP

How do the seasons of Joshua's life encourage you in your own?

93

Time to Get Intolerant

Judges 1:1-36

What are you tolerating in your life? You know, that *thing* you put up with because it's not worth the fight?

It can be as simple as your toddler's choice of wardrobe—sure, the explosion of patterns *does not match*, **but hey, they dressed themselves!** Or maybe it's your spouse's quirks—their ways of loading the dishwasher, folding towels, and clipping their toenails are cringe, but you know what, **at least they're cleaning up**. Or maybe it's a bigger deal—you're tolerating an unhealthy habit or a toxic relationship, or you're sweeping a seemingly small sin under the rug.

After Joshua died, the Israelites were charged with one task: Drive out the Canaanites. Yet back-to-back, we read the same refrain with each tribe (italics added):

Judah: "*Failed to drive out* the people living in the plains, who had iron chariots" (Judges 1:19)

Benjamin: "*Failed to drive out* the Jebusites . . . to this day the Jebusites live" among them (1:21)

Manasseh: "*Failed to drive out the people* . . . because the Canaanites were determined to stay" (1:27-28)
Ephraim: "*Failed to drive out* the Canaanites" (1:29)
Zebulun: "*Failed to drive out* the residents" (1:30)
Asher: "*Failed to drive out* the residents" (1:31)
Naphtali: "*Failed to drive out* the residents . . . instead, they moved in among the Canaanites, who controlled the land" (1:33)
Dan: "The Amorites *forced them back* into the hill country and would not let them come down into the plains" (1:34)

It got to the point that the "angel of the LORD"—Jesus Himself—confronted them: "You were not to make any covenants with the people living in this land; instead, you were to destroy their altars. But you disobeyed my command. Why did you do this?" (Judges 2:1-2).

Like a loving parent wanting only what's best for us, He's still asking that question today: *Why are you doing this?*

Because if we're honest, as Jesus offers the free, abundant life, we sometimes sin instead. We tolerate the presence of the enemy versus driving it out. We move in among our culture's norms and immerse ourselves in its ways. And at times, we allow the world to dictate how we live. Since, hey, what's really the big deal?

But if we continue down the same path as the Israelites, permitting our enemies to stay and influence us, they will be "thorns in your sides, and their gods will be a constant temptation to you" (Judges 2:3).

Good news for us: We don't have to settle for less than God's best. We can change course, push back the darkness, and welcome the clean slate with new mercies in Jesus Christ *today*.

Instead of failure's refrain, in His name and by His power, we can succeed, thrive, and flourish. But the choice is yours—will you settle for halfsies . . . or will you go *all in*?

TAKE THE NEXT STEP

What might you be tolerating that is keeping you from basking in your free, abundant life?

Whether bitterness, hopelessness, an unhealthy habit, or a wayward obsession, make haste to expel it, banish it, and show it the door. Freedom is, most certainly, on the other side.

94

Not on Your Watch

Judges 2:6-13

Were you raised in a Christian home?

I'm gonna be honest, this has become one of my favorite blessings. Not because I grew up with DC Talk (**although it didn't hurt!**) but because my parents gave me a front-row seat to what a personal relationship with Jesus looks like. From an early age, I saw how much they loved church, and I remember flipping through the well-loved pages of their Bibles. They prayed with us before meals and bedtime. They gave generously, and I saw how God gave more generously.

This overflow of faith from one generation to the next *matters*—**both for us now and back in Joshua's day too.** For "the Israelites served the LORD throughout the lifetime of Joshua. . . . Another generation grew up who did not acknowledge the LORD or remember the mighty things he had done for Israel" (Judges 2:7, 10).

This isn't the only time that happened. Fast-forward to 2 Kings, and after generations had left God's Temple in disrepair, a young boy of a king started renovations. The priest heading up the DIY project stumbled upon a book inside, and King Josiah's secretary began reading it to him. After hearing God's Word, Josiah "tore his robes"—not as a weird fashion statement, but out of great despair (2 Kings 22:11). Immediately seeking God "because those who have gone before us have not obeyed the words of this book" (verse 13, NIV), he wanted to make things right.

Too often, though, we buy into the lie that because faith is personal, it's also private. But nowhere does the Bible say that. Rather, it repeatedly warns of what happens when we shirk the responsibility of teaching the next generation about Him.

Sure, they might profess faith when we're around, and they might go to church when everyone dutifully attends on holidays, but when they stand before God someday, will they know Him as Lord and Savior? Uff da, I know. IT'S HEAVY. But it's worth calling out now before it's too late . . .

For every believer, this is it. This is what life is about. Jesus has entrusted us with His mission to *go out* and *speak up* about what He has done for us. "Tell it to your children, and let your children tell it to their children, and their children to the next generation" (Joel 1:3, NIV).

But it will involve opening our mouths. Sharing the hope within us. Repeating the ways God has moved in our lives. Otherwise, "how can they believe in him if they have never heard about him? . . . And how can they hear about him unless *someone tells them*?" (Romans 10:14, italics added).

Today, let's part ways with the Israelites' example. Whether in our homes, at youth group, or in classrooms, how about you and I teach the next generation about our good God? He will take it from there, sending ripples out through our children's children and into the lives of *their* children's children.

TAKE THE NEXT STEP

Who is within your sphere of influence? How can you share about God with the next generation?

Whether around the dinner table, in the car, or on the phone, tell them about an answered prayer. Retell a Bible story you read today. And pray, pray, pray as long as you have breath.

95

Who Has the Upper Hand—You or Your Problems?

Judges 1:1-36

What giants still dwell in the landscape of your life?

I don't mean to pry (or maybe I do), but I only ask because this is one of the main reasons I wrote this book. For me, no matter how long I had been in remission, the same monstrous giant rose up to darken my days with its ever-looming shadow.

When yet another new set of symptoms flared up, the stress bubbled to its boiling point. Reaching my end, I cried out to the Lord, "I believe you give the free, abundant life—so why do I feel completely *hammered down*, *dominated* by health threats, and *enslaved* to constantly 'staying on top of things' with no end in sight?"

Turns out I'm not the only one who's given my giants the upper hand. By letting the Canaanites stay in the land, the Israelites began sliding down a slippery slope. In a matter of verses, we read "a significant change in phraseology"[3]—no longer was it "the Canaanites lived among them" but now, God's people, the Asherites, "lived among the Canaanite inhabitants" (Judges 1:30, 32, NIV).

Do you see the switch-up? **I almost missed it too.** Where God's people once had the advantage, it turned into the enemy's dominance *over* *them* with even "stronger resistance." It escalated to the point that these Canaanite strongholds kept Israel from being able "to move about freely."[4]

Fast-forward to the time of the judges, and the Israelites began succumbing to the widespread dominance of another Canaanite giant, the Philistines, tempted to give up their hope of freedom altogether. So much so that when Samson rose up against what _*he thought*_ was their common enemy, three thousand Israelites turned on *him* in indignation: "Don't you realize that the Philistines are rulers over us?" (Judges 15:11).

As if fighting back was now unthinkable. Taboo. Even offensive? Better to give up on God's reign today because *this is just how it is.*

These men became so convinced of these lies that they tied up Samson—their own God-given judge, warrior, and *deliverer*—and hand-delivered him to their enemy instead.

This is when I felt God point out that by allowing fear to reign today, I'm only giving it permission to dominate now and tomorrow. By tolerating anxiety in this scenario, I allow it to grow and give it the upper hand for future situations too. By permitting my mind to dwell on worst-case scenarios, I'm limiting my own freedom. But I don't have to put up with it any longer. In Jesus' name, I must drive it out without delay.

Maybe it's finally time you did the same.

TAKE THE NEXT STEP

Where do you feel unable to move about freely, restricted in your thoughts, or tormented by the presence of darkness?

Good news: There's no need to give the giants your blessing to remain on the landscape of your life any longer. Let's drive them out today before they grow and dominate.

If ______, Then ______

Judges 2

What are some if-then scenarios you've run across lately?

Maybe at work—*if* sales exceed the target, *then* you get a bonus. Or with personal goals? *If* you run X amount of miles, *then* you splurge on new shoes. *If* you pass an exam, *then* treat yo'self to Starbucks.

Or possibly with the kids, just your average, "*If* you clean your room, *then* you can have screen time" or "*If* you make another poop joke at the table, *then* mama bear's coming out (and it's not to defend her cubs)." JK . . . kinda.

When God ushered His people into the Promised Land, He gave His own if-then condition through Moses: "Keep his decrees and commands . . . so that it may go well with you and your children after you and that you may live long in the land" (Deuteronomy 4:40, NIV).

Did you know *we* are given conditional promises as well? The word *if* is used 574 times in the New Testament, often by Jesus Himself.[5]

> "If you keep My commandments, you will remain in My love" (John 15:10, NASB).
>
> "If we confess our sins, he is faithful and just and will forgive us our sins" (1 John 1:9, NIV).
>
> "If you believe, you will see the glory of God" (John 11:40, NIV).

Don't get me wrong. Some of God's best promises are unconditional, and there's nothing you can do to earn salvation, His love, or His forgiveness. He offers them *freely* to *all who believe.*

But if we want fullness of joy, it's found by spending time in God's presence (Psalm 16:11). If we want to abound in hope, we must seek the God of hope (Romans 15:13). If we want peace, we're to tell God what we need and thank Him for all He has done (Philippians 4:6). Essentially, if we want the free, abundant life, we need only to seek Jesus, the Life-Giving Fountain (Psalm 36:9).

For the Israelites, the charge was clear. Obey to remain. Disobey and things go south, your time cut short. But it was more than just obedience. To live in the land is to love the God of the land, for there is no life apart from Him. But the Israelites chose the road apart from Him time and again—and filled the whole book of Judges with the consequences.

But you and I are not them, and I'm declaring for both of us, ***our path will be different***. We are people of God, who love Jesus, live in the light, and run in the path of His commands. We follow the Way and bear the fruit of the Spirit. We drive out the enemies when they encroach on our territory. And "if we endure, we will also reign with him" (2 Timothy 2:12, NIV).

The Landlord is generously offering the deed to the whole land, and it's *all yours*. So how about we put down roots, abide by the family rules, and make ourselves at home?

TAKE THE NEXT STEP

What if-then condition most stands out to you today?

When you meet a hindrance to the abundant life in Christ, remember this is your Promised Land. "Neither death nor life, neither angels nor demons, neither our fears for today nor our worries about tomorrow—not even the powers of hell can separate us from God's love" (Romans 8:38).

97

Three Different Stages

Judges 3:1-5

What stage of life are you in?

Maybe you're fresh out of college, single as a Pringle and ready to mingle, and learning the (**lame**) art of adulting. Possibly you're at midlife, tending to your family, advancing your career, or still waiting on your calling. Or maybe you're an empty nester, adjusting to a new norm.

As we've stalked the Israelites through the Promised Land, have you, too, picked up on how they cycled through three different life stages?

1. **Battling.** The land was theirs, but the call was to seize it. So going head-to-head with their enemies, God's people confronted walls meant to block them, passed through waters obstructing their way, and picked up arms with stretches of back-to-back battles for *years.*
2. **Compromising.** They were warned to "be very careful to love the Lord your God" and "drive out all the people living there . . . destroy all their carved and molten images" (Joshua 23:11; Numbers 33:52). Yet they befriended their neighbors, and between meeting up for drinks or playdates, they fell into the enemy's trap.
3. **Resting.** While others were discontented with their lot, eyeing their brothers' land, some, like Caleb and Joshua, looked at the blessing they were given, and with a heart of gratitude, rested in it.

If I'm totally honest, on day 1 of this devotional, I would've said I was compromising. Not in the sense of giving in to "the lust of the flesh, the lust of the eyes, and the pride of life" (1 John 2:16, NIV), the usual connotation of that word.

I just mean I was exhausted from the battle being waged in my mind. With each follow-up test, new symptom, and ominous word from a doctor, the what-ifs swirled in my thoughts and began to dominate. After years of continually driving them out, I gradually stopped fighting. I let the giant of threatening cancer stay in the landscape of my life. I inadvertently accepted its presence, shackled myself in fear, and suffered the consequences.

Realizing this, I said to the Lord, "I may have compromised yesterday, but today, I'm fighting—and by the end of this devotional book, I pray and hope to be resting in You again."

I'm happy to say a lot of days, I'm resting in the bliss of His presence and the abundant life He gives. Other days, I cycle through all three stages in twenty-four hours. But I told my husband, "I must be gaining ground because even when I fall into compromise in a moment of panic, I spring back into battle mode faster. I enter into His presence sooner and am enveloped in His peace, sometimes within moments."

No matter what stage you are in, I hope you know that in Christ, the cycle always ends in rest. You may be exhausted from fighting an uphill battle or tolerating giants of your own, but Jesus invites you this very moment: "Come to me, all you who are weary and burdened, and I will give you rest" (Matthew 11:28, NIV). How about we take Him up on His offer, kick up our feet in this spot, and *stay awhile*?

TAKE THE NEXT STEP

Which stage of the Promised Land would you say you're currently dwelling in?

How can you see your blessings for what they are—gifts from the God of the land—and thank Him for them?

98

Drive Out the Giants

Judges 3:5-6

What would you say is your biggest enemy to date? Let's name it.

If the Promised Land is one big metaphor for our free, abundant life in Christ, then the seven enemies of the Israelites hold just as much symbolism.

A smart dude in the seventeenth century by the name of Thomas Bromley wrote "The Seven Nations of Canaan, which Joshua cast out, prefiguring the Works of Jesus, casting out the evil Properties they signify, out of our Souls." **(You know, keepin' it short and sweet.)** He emphasized that it's worth familiarizing ourselves not only with what each enemy represents, but also with how the Israelites drove them out so we can follow suit.[6]

Hittites. Translated "sons of terror," these giants can "discourage the soul continually with false fears." But having the mind of Christ, we can fight that spirit of fear in the Spirit of "power and of love and of a sound mind" (1 Corinthians 2:16; 2 Timothy 1:7, NKJV).

Girgashites. Meaning "clay dweller," they built their houses on the material things of this world. But those who build their house on the Rock, the "precious cornerstone, of a sure foundation" (Isaiah 28:16, ESV), will not fall.

Amorites. This nation signifies "bitter fierce-talking and judging." But we overcome by getting "rid of all bitterness, rage, anger, harsh words, and slander" and by letting our words be "good and helpful" and "an encouragement to those who hear them" (Ephesians 4:29, 31).

Canaanites. These guys symbolize "spirits that traffic in our minds, wills, thoughts, senses, imaginations, and affections," opposing "holy silence and pure stillness." But instead of getting caught up in the speed of this world or polluting our minds with information overload, we can "be still in the presence of the LORD, and wait patiently for him to act" (Psalm 37:7).

Perizzites. These people lived in unprotected, unwalled villages, yet the "first mention of them is in connection with cramped living space." Without God's good boundaries, you'll find yourself constricted by the sin of lawlessness (1 John 3:4). We need only to realize "the lines have fallen for me in pleasant places; indeed, I have a beautiful inheritance" (Psalm 16:6, ESV).

Hivites. They led a luxurious lifestyle, seemingly living by "if it feels good, do it" and "look out for number one." But instead of pursuing comfort and our own gain, we prevail when we offer ourselves as a living sacrifice (Romans 12:1).

Jebusites. With a name meaning "thresher" and to trample underfoot, these people personify pride, stomping on others to elevate themselves. Instead of seeking fame, being right, or the approval of others, we can overcome by seeking the pleasure of God above all else (James 4:6; Galatians 1:10).

If you let these giants run rampant, they'll dominate, as the Israelites showed us. But God wants to "push them out for your sake" (Joshua 23:5, NIV). ***Your call.*** He will show us a way out of every temptation, so that we can endure . . . and ultimately, overcome (1 Corinthians 10:13). How about we take Him up on that offer this very day?

TAKE THE NEXT STEP

Which of these giants do you need to drive out?

Memorize the accompanying verse, and fight back with the Sword of the Spirit, the Word of God.

99

Trading This Overarching Lie for the Freeing Truth

Judges 3:9

What do you want above all else? Maybe it's tangible—a new house or job. Or maybe it's abstract—a renewed relationship or peace of mind.

When God's people first entered the Promised Land, they followed their leader and prophet, Joshua, as he spoke the Word of God to His people. They were set. But when Joshua passed away and the Israelites became dominated by the Canaanites, they cried out to God for help and "the LORD raised up a rescuer to save them" (Judges 3:9). "Whenever the LORD raised up a judge over Israel, he was with that judge and rescued the people from their enemies. . . . But when the judge died, the people returned to their corrupt ways, behaving worse than those who had lived before them" (Judges 2:18-19).

After twelve judges, the Israelites were *over it.*

They demanded a king to go out before them and fight their battles so they could "be like the nations around us" (1 Samuel 8:20). Samuel warned how kings reign—drafting sons into war, forcing daughters into labor, taking the best of the land for his officials, demanding the finest of their flock as a tax. "When that day comes, you will beg for relief from this king you are demanding" (verse 18). But these people refused to listen: "Even so, we still want a king" (verse 19).

We aren't that different, are we? We still want that certain relationship, that big break in our career, a great leap in our finances, more clothes in our closet, more food in our bellies, more followers on social media—even if it's not for our best. Because we've already convinced ourselves, of course it is.

But every one of our wants is meant to point us to Jesus, and every need can be met in Him.

Better than Joshua, He is the ultimate Leader, the Commander of the army of the Lord (Joshua 5:14).

Better than the former prophets, He is the Prophet, who not only spoke the Word, but *is* the Word (Mark 6:4; John 1:1).

Better than any judge, He is our Rescuer, Savior, and Judge—***also a title for Messiah and God*** (Isaiah 19:20; Isaiah 43:11).

Finally, better than all kings combined, He is the King of kings and Lord of lords, reigning forever (Revelation 11:15).

No matter where we stand in the Land of Promise, we don't have to chase after things to fulfill us or people to lead us. We can simply "seek first his kingdom and his righteousness" (Matthew 6:33, NIV), and *everything else* will fall into place.

Truly, Jesus is all we need, and in Him, we lack *nothing*.

TAKE THE NEXT STEP

Fill in the blank: If I had ______________, then I'd be fulfilled.

Go straight to Jesus in prayer and trade this lie for the truth: Only He "is able to bless you abundantly, so that in all things at all times, having all that you need, you will abound in every good work" (2 Corinthians 9:8, NIV).

100

The Pure Land of Promise Is Coming

Revelation 21:4

How many homes have you had so far?

Including my parents' houses, my college dorm, and the apartment Ty and I hunkered down in for a year, my tally is up to ten. But **lemme be cliché in a way that would make Hobby Lobby proud**: None of them has felt like home unless I've been with my family.

Here's the final thing we have to realize as we approach the finish line: Once the Israelites were laying down roots and welcome mats in their new homes, it was no longer the land of Canaan. As they "settled there . . . the LORD gave them rest on every side" (Joshua 21:44, NIV), this was now the Land of Promise.

The same is true for you. We were once under the dominant hand of sin with the enemy running rampant in our lives. But the landscape has changed. Jesus has freed us and empowered us. We are now God's children, given His inheritance and deemed "more than conquerors through him who loved us" (Romans 8:37, NIV). In Him, we find rest on every side.

Yet make no mistake: Giants will still attempt to dwell in our backyard. Battles are still on the horizon. And sin is still in the picture because "this world is not our permanent home" (Hebrews 13:14).

But our giants have an end date. A day is coming when Jesus will return, creating a new heaven and earth and resurrecting our souls. Free from taunting giants, towering walls, and raging waters, this is the "better country—a heavenly one" (Hebrews 11:16, NIV), the homeland Jesus is preparing for you *right now*.

In this world, we may bounce from house to house, battle to battle, season to season. But as a citizen of heaven, you can look forward to your permanent home, the ultimate resting spot, where the Lord Himself will "wipe every tear from [your] eyes, and there will be no more death or sorrow or crying or pain" (Revelation 21:4). ***And we'll never have to move again.***

It'll be *home*—not because of where it is but Who we're with. Jesus Himself will dwell with us! This is our ultimate inheritance "kept in heaven for you, pure and undefiled, beyond the reach of change and decay" (1 Peter 1:4). The Land of Promise of today is merely a hint of the pure Land of Promise of tomorrow.

In the meantime, know for certain that "our light and momentary troubles are achieving for us an eternal glory that far outweighs them all. So we fix our eyes not on what is seen, but on what is unseen, since what is seen is temporary, but what is unseen is eternal. For we know that . . . we have a building from God, an eternal house in heaven" (2 Corinthians 4:17–5:1, NIV).

Go *all in* in this world because the pure Land of Promise with its streets of gold is *all yours* . . . surely, home sweet home.

TAKE THE NEXT STEP

In light of the heavenly home waiting for you, how can you fix your eyes on what is unseen versus seen?

Let the reality of your future home help you take a tangible next step today. Remember to seek first the Lord, His Kingdom, and His righteousness—and everything else will fall into place (Matthew 6:33).

ULTIMATE TRUTHS
in the Promised Land

You are the servant of the Lord

You don't work for victory, but from it

It's time to be intolerant of sin

Teach the next generation about your God

Drive out the remaining opposition before it grows + dominates

To live in the land is to love the God of the land

Battles may come, but you can always rest in Christ

God will provide a way for you to endure + overcome

God will meet all of your needs + in Him, you lack nothing

You are a citizen of heaven

YOU DID IT.

UFF DA, one hundred days, done and complete. Can you even believe it? I don't care if you sped through in three months or dragged it out to three years, goodness gracious, cue up Kool & the Gang and let's **CELEBRATE GOOD TIMES, COME ON.**

I hate goodbyes, so here's how we're gonna wrap up: Check out the map of the Promised Land to see where the Israelites finally ended up. Remember, when we first began, these people hadn't even set a *foot* inside their territory yet. It took time. And it required faith.

But now look. Across mountaintops and through valleys, past the river's crest and once-fortressed walls, beyond the desert and barren patches, they have arrived. The land overflowing with milk and honey, the Land of Promise, the land their good God gave to them was *all theirs*.

The same is true for us. We may have started off this journey with our toes at the edge of the Promised Land, unsure how to seize the abundant life, and desperately wanting to live in the freedom Christ gives. But step-by-step, we learned more of God's promises and took Him up on His Word. We persevered through our own fights. We pushed the giants out of the landscape of our lives. Essentially, we went *all in*.

And look where you stand now . . . resting in the free, abundant life Christ wanted to give you all along. **#blessed**

Never forget it: Go all in because it's all yours.

Father, thank You for Your Son and His sacrifice, for adopting us into Your family, and for taking our dead hearts and giving us new life. Surely, we now know, "the land you have given [us] is a pleasant land. What a wonderful inheritance!" (Psalm 16:6). Jesus, You are the Way. Thanks for showing the way! We want all that You have for us, so lead on, Good Shepherd. We're right on Your heels, ready for it all, excited for the land overflowing with milk and honey. We love You! In Jesus' powerful name we pray, amen.

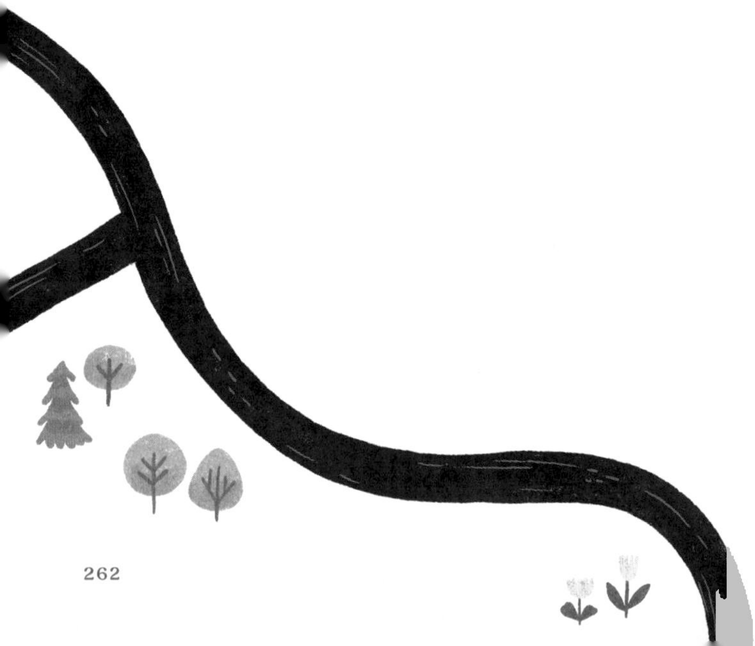

Journaling Pages

Notes

LET'S HIT THE ROAD, JACK— ER, RATHER *(INSERT YOUR NAME HERE)*

1. Lenya Heitzig and Penny Pierce Rose, *Live Fearlessly: A Study in the Book of Joshua*, vol. 2 (David C. Cook, 2018), 39.
2. Hey, if you missed the "original," no need to suffer FOMO any longer. Just tell Goodreads my first book, *P.S. It's Gonna Be Good* (Tyndale House, 2023), is next on your list.

MILEPOST 1: KNOW WHAT YOU'RE STEPPING INTO

1. "Why Is Joshua Called 'Jesus' in Hebrews 4:8 in the KJV?" Got Questions, accessed February 26, 2025, https://www.gotquestions.org/Joshua-Jesus.html.
2. Martin H. Manser, ed., *Zondervan Dictionary of Bible Themes* (Zondervan, 1999).
3. Anne Lamott, *Traveling Mercies: Some Thoughts on Faith* (Anchor Books, 2000), 239.
4. Bill Gaultiere, "Chew Your Cud on God's Word," Soul Shepherding, accessed February 26, 2025, https://www.soulshepherding.org/chew-your-cud-on-gods-word/.

MILEPOST 2: GET YO'SELF READY

1. Russell McKinney, "Choosing the East Side of the Jordan," *The Disciple's Road* (blog), February 6, 2019, https://russellmckinney.com/2019/02/06/choosing-the-east-side-of-the-jordan/.
2. Robert Smith Jr., *Christ-Centered Exposition Commentary: Exalting Jesus in Joshua* (B&H Publishing Group, 2023), 33.

3. C. S. Lewis to Mary Willis Shelburne, June 17, 1963, in *Narnia, Cambridge, and Joy 1950–1963*, ed. Walter Hooper, vol. 3, *The Collected Letters of C.S. Lewis*, (HarperCollins, 2007), 1430.
4. Heidi Lee Anderson, *P.S. It's Gonna Be Good: How God's Word Answers Our Questions about Faith, Fear, and All the Things* (Tyndale House, 2023), 118.
5. John Gray, *Joshua, Judges, Ruth* (HarperCollins, 1986), 63.
6. Paul P. Enns, *Joshua* (Zondervan, 1981), 28.
7. Dictionary.com, "demolish (*v.*)," accessed October 10, 2024, https://www.dictionary.com/browse/demolish.
8. Barb Roose, *Joshua: Winning the Worry Battle* (Abingdon, 2018), 55.
9. Enns, *Joshua*, 34.
10. Lenya Heitzig and Penny Pierce Rose, *Live Fearlessly: A Study in the Book of Joshua*, vol. 2 (David C. Cook, 2018), 62.

MILEPOST 3: LET'S MOVE OUT

1. Paul P. Enns, *Joshua* (Zondervan, 1981), 36.
2. Encyclopedia.com, "consecrate," accessed October 21, 2024, https://www.encyclopedia.com/literature-and-arts/language-linguistics-and-literary-terms/english-vocabulary-d/consecrate.
3. Carl Friedrich Keil and Franz Delitzsch, "Commentary on Joshua 3," *Keil & Delitzsch Old Testament Commentary*, accessed February 26, 2025, https://www.studylight.org/commentaries/eng/kdo/joshua-3.html.
4. Enns, *Joshua*, 39.
5. Kyle Idleman quoted in Heidi Lee Anderson, *P.S. It's Gonna Be Good: How God's Word Answers Our Questions about Faith, Fear, and All the Things* (Tyndale House, 2023), 126.
6. Anderson, *P.S. It's Gonna Be Good*, 133.

MILEPOST 4: NORMAL VS. UNUSUAL BATTLE STRATEGY

1. Heidi Lee Anderson, *P.S. It's Gonna Be Good: How God's Word Answers Our Questions about Faith, Fear, and All the Things* (Tyndale House, 2023), 125.
2. Paul P. Enns, *Joshua* (Zondervan, 1981), 58.
3. Steven Curtis Chapman, "Dive," track 1 on *Speechless*, Sparrow Records, 1999.
4. WordReference.com, "devoted (*adj.*)," accessed October 26, 2024, https://www.wordreference.com/definition/devoted.
5. Merriam-Webster, "honor (*n.*)," accessed December 30, 2024, https://www.merriam-webster.com/dictionary/honor.

6. John MacArthur, *Joshua, Judges, and Ruth: Finally in the Land* (Thomas Nelson, 2016), 39.
7. Fran Simone, "Negative Self-Talk: Don't Let It Overwhelm You," *Psychology Today*, December 4, 2017, https://www.psychologytoday.com/us/blog/family-affair/201712/negative-self-talk-dont-let-it-overwhelm-you.
8. Simone, "Negative Self-Talk."
9. Lenya Heitzig and Penny Rose, *Live Fearlessly: A Study in the Book of Joshua* (David C. Cook, 2008), 159.
10. David Guzik, "Joshua 8—Victory over Ai, Israel at Gerizim and Ebal," *Enduring Word Bible Commentary*, accessed February 26, 2025, https://enduringword.com/bible-commentary/joshua-8/.

MILEPOST 5: ENEMIES MUST BOW DOWN

1. Paul P. Enns, *Joshua* (Zondervan, 1981), 84.
2. John MacArthur, *Joshua, Judges, and Ruth: Finally in the Land* (Thomas Nelson, 2016), 52.
3. Response to "How long would it take a well-trained military unit to march 25 miles?," ChatGPT, Open AI, October 27, 2024.
4. Enns, *Joshua*, 84.
5. Craig Groeschel, "What you pray about reflects what you believe about God," Facebook, June 1, 2019, https://www.facebook.com/photo.php?fbid=2348782255180345&id=104547962937130&set=a.119436738114919.
6. Barb Roose, *Joshua: Winning the Worry Battle* (Abingdon, 2018), 130.
7. Enns, *Joshua*, 85.
8. Robert Smith Jr., *Christ-Centered Exposition Commentary: Exalting Jesus in Joshua* (B&H Publishing Group, 2023), 144.
9. Lenya Heitzig and Penny Rose, *Live Fearlessly: A Study in the Book of Joshua* (David C. Cook, 2008), 212.
10. "Malachi 4:3," Benson Commentary, Bible Hub, accessed February 26, 2025, https://biblehub.com/commentaries/malachi/4-3.htm.

MILEPOST 6: FINISH STRONG

1. Paul. P. Enns, *Joshua* (Zondervan, 1981), 88.
2. Enns, *Joshua*, 91.
3. Barb Roose, *Joshua: Winning the Worry Battle* (Abingdon, 2018), 137.
4. Dale Ralph Davis, *Joshua: No Falling Words* (Christian Focus, 2012), quoted in Robert Smith Jr., *Christ-Centered Exposition Commentary: Exalting Jesus in Joshua* (B&H Publishing Group, 2023), 149.

5. Enns, *Joshua*, 95–96.
6. John MacArthur, *Joshua, Judges, and Ruth: Finally in the Land* (Thomas Nelson, 2016), 57.
7. "Joshua 11:4," Gill's Exposition of the Entire Bible, Bible Hub, accessed February 26, 2025, https://biblehub.com/commentaries/joshua/11-4.htm.
8. Enns, *Joshua*, 96.
9. Enns, *Joshua*, 99.

MILEPOST 7: POST-BATTLE ANALYSIS

1. Robert Smith Jr., *Christ-Centered Exposition Commentary: Exalting Jesus in Joshua* (B&H Publishing Group, 2023), 157.
2. Adapted from Jason Strand, "No Longer I," Eagle Brook Church, May 26, 2024, 19:28, https://www.eaglebrookchurch.com/media/past-messages/no-longer-i/.
3. Strand, "No Longer I," 20:05.
4. "Strong's H5857," Blue Letter Bible, accessed February 26, 2025, https://www.blueletterbible.org/lexicon/h5857/kjv/wlc/0-1/. Also see Joshua 8:1, 28.
5. "Strong's H3389," Blue Letter Bible, accessed February 26, 2025, https://www.blueletterbible.org/lexicon/h3389/kjv/wlc/0-1/. Also see Joshua 10:1-8.
6. "Strong's H5725," Blue Letter Bible, accessed February 26, 2025, https://www.blueletterbible.org/lexicon/h5725/kjv/wlc/0-1/.
7. "Strong's H3412," Blue Letter Bible, accessed February 26, 2025, https://www.blueletterbible.org/lexicon/h3412/kjv/wlc/0-1/. Also see Joshua 10:1-8.
8. "Strong's H1445," Blue Letter Bible, accessed February 26, 2025, https://www.blueletterbible.org/lexicon/h1445/kjv/wlc/0-1/. Also see Joshua 12:13.
9. "Strong's H663," Blue Letter Bible, accessed February 26, 2025, https://www.blueletterbible.org/lexicon/h663/kjv/wlc/0-1/.
10. C. H. Spurgeon, "Taking Possession of Our Inheritance," sermon, May 12, 1889, Metropolitan Tabernacle, Newington, https://www.blueletterbible.org/comm/spurgeon_charles/sermons/2086.cfm; italics added.
11. Gregg Hunter, "Claiming Ephraim and Manasseh (Genesis 48:1-9)," *Fort Howard Community Church* (blog), July 21, 2021, https://www.forthowardcc.com/blog/post/claiming-ephraim-and-manasseh--genesis-481-9-.

MILEPOST 8: PLOTLINES OF PURPOSE

1. Paul P. Enns, *Joshua* (Zondervan, 1981), 115.
2. Lenya Heitzig and Penny Rose, *Live Fearlessly: A Study in the Book of Joshua* (David C. Cook, 2008), 271.

3. David Guzik, "Genesis 49—The Blessing of the Sons of Jacob," Enduring Word Commentary, accessed February 26, 2025, https://enduringword.com/bible-commentary/genesis-49/.
4. Heitzig and Rose, *Live Fearlessly*, 288.
5. Heitzig and Rose, *Live Fearlessly*, 284.
6. Heitzig and Rose, *Live Fearlessly*, 284.
7. "God So Loved," by Andrew Bergthold et al., on We the Kingdom, *Holy Water*, Capitol CMG Publishing, 2019.
8. Kelly Minter, *Finding God Faithful: A Study on the Life of Joseph* (Lifeway, 2019), 46.
9. Steven Furtick, "Triggered: Taking Back Your Mind in the Age of Anxiety, Part 6," sermon, Elevation Church, posted October 1, 2018, video, 53:30, https://www.youtube.com/watch?v=Mi80NIttniU.
10. Robert Smith Jr., *Christ-Centered Exposition Commentary: Exalting Jesus in Joshua* (B&H Publishing Group, 2023), 189.
11. Barb Roose, *Joshua: Winning the Worry Battle* (Abingdon, 2018), 166.
12. Smith, *Exalting Jesus in Joshua*, 197.
13. Tommi Waters, "Zebulun of the Bible: Overview, History & Tribes," Study.com, updated November 21, 2023, https://study.com/academy/lesson/tribe-of-zebulun-history-symbol-characteristics.html#:~:text=Their%20territory%20bordered%20both%20the,how%20they%20made%20their%20money.
14. Susan J. Nelson, "Tribe of Asher in the Bible & 2 Lessons We Can Learn," *Woman of Noble Character* (blog), July 5, 2024, https://www.womanofnoblecharacter.com/tribe-of-asher/.
15. "The Allotment for Naphtali," Bible Hub, accessed February 26, 2025, https://biblehub.com/topical/t/the_allotment_for_naphtali.htm.
16. Mike Pettengill, "Blessed to Be a Blessing," The Gospel Coalition, April 17, 2013, https://www.thegospelcoalition.org/article/blessed-to-be-a-blessing/.
17. Roose, *Joshua*, 179.
18. "Joshua 19:50," Cambridge Bible for Schools and Colleges, BibleHub, accessed February 26, 2025, https://biblehub.com/commentaries/joshua/19-50.htm.
19. Smith, *Exalting Jesus in Joshua*, 195.

MILEPOST 9: GATHER AROUND FOR SOME FATHERLY ADVICE

1. Heidi Lee Anderson, *P.S. It's Gonna Be Good: How God's Word Answers Our Questions about Faith, Fear, and All the Things* (Tyndale, 2023), 90, 91, 94–95.
2. *Merriam-Webster Dictionary*, "allotted (*adj.*)," accessed November 12, 2024, https://www.merriam-webster.com/dictionary/allotted.

3. *Cambridge Dictionary*, "allotted (*adj.*)," accessed November 12, 2024, https://dictionary.cambridge.org/us/dictionary/english/allotted.
4. Kyle Idleman, "7 Days of Victory," sermon, Southeast Christian Church, March 28, 2021, video, 1:23:48, https://www.youtube.com/watch?v=KNEN9feRGvA.
5. "PRK (Photorefractive Keratectomy)," Flaum Eye Institute, University of Rochester Medical Center, accessed December 28, 2024, https://www.urmc.rochester.edu/eye-institute/lasik/procedures/prk.aspx.
6. Interview with John Piper, "Following Christ Is Costly—But How Do You Count the Cost?" *Ask Pastor John*, January 29, 2018, https://www.desiringgod.org/interviews/following-christ-is-costly-but-how-do-you-count-the-cost.
7. Rachel Glik, "Retelling Family Stories: Secret Benefits and Tips for Sharing Them," *Dr. Rachel Glik* (blog), November 19, 2020, https://www.drrachelglik.com/blog-posts/2020/11/19/retelling-family-stories-secret-benefits-and-tips-for-sharing-them.
8. Interview with John Piper, "What Is an Idol?" *Ask Pastor John*, January 3, 2022, https://www.desiringgod.org/interviews/what-is-an-idol.

MILEPOST 10: TRUTHS TO TAKE WITH YOU INTO THE PROMISED LAND

1. "What Does It Mean to Be a Servant of Christ?" Got Questions, updated January 4, 2022, https://www.gotquestions.org/servant-of-Christ.html.
2. Heidi Lee Anderson, *P.S. It's Gonna Be Good: How God's Word Answers Our Questions about Faith, Fear, and All the Things* (Tyndale, 2023), 124.
3. Paul P. Enns, *Judges* (Zondervan, 1982), 29.
4. Enns, *Judges*, 29, 30.
5. Rex Rouis, "If—The Biggest Word in the Bible," HopeFaithPrayer, accessed February 26, 2025, https://www.hopefaithprayer.com/biggest-word-bible/.
6. The following information on the enemy nations was gathered from these sources: Edward V. Beck, "Seven Nations and Seven Purgings to Spiritual Perfection," *Sober Souls* (blog), November 28, 2015, http://sobersouls.blogspot.com/2015/11/seven-nations-and-seven-purgings-to.html; and "The Seven Enemies of Israel in the Promised Land," Bible Fellowship Union, http://www.biblefellowshipunion.co.uk/2014/Sep_Oct/7Enemies.htm.

ACKNOWLEDGMENTS

1. Heidi Lee Anderson, *P.S. It's Gonna Be Good: How God's Word Answers Our Questions about Faith, Fear, and All the Things* (Tyndale, 2023), 270.

Topical Index

Acknowledgments

There's one Person who's walked me through the uncertain terrain of college, seen me through challenges as a ministry leader, and held my hand during chemotherapy as a cancer patient. He's the same Person who excitedly introduced me to Ty, generously blessed us with children, and opened doors online and in person to share His Word. He's the One who strengthens me each morning, fills my days with purpose, and watches over me every night. His Name is Jesus, and He deserves all praise and glory and honor. Thank You, Lord, for Your sovereignty, guidance, help, and victory over my life. You're the reason my hope's never lost, and I'll love You forever.

Ty, this year, we (somehow) wrote a book, started a church group, sold a house, moved, built a house—all while still working, loving our kids, and sending weird cat reels to each other. It wasn't easy (and the stain snafu certainly put me over the edge), but Owl City still rings true: "We don't even have to try . . . it's always a good time." You're the real MVP and my Ephesians 3:20 proof that God indeed does "immeasurably more than all we ask or imagine" (NIV). The best is yet to come!

Oscar, Mabel, Hazel, and Dottie, so much of what I do, I do for you—this book included. More than anything, I desperately want you to know Jesus is the only Way, so someday when you grow up, I hope these books of mine find their way into your hands. When this one does, don't miss the parts about how much your God loves you, has good plans for you, and will never leave you nor abandon you. Above all else, keep the faith, okay? It'll change everything . . . because He will change everything.

Mom and Dad, from *P.S. It's Gonna Be Good*, I quote, "Practically speaking—without you (Mom) watching the kids each week, this book wouldn't have happened . . . probably should've dedicated this to you, LOL."[1] Better late than never, right? This one's for you! Love you guys—thanks over and over again.

Tammy and Gordy, while this book was being made, you painted, sanded, and brought our kids ice cream. So since I dedicated this book to my parents, it only seems fair I dedicate our new house to you. Deal? Love you both!

My grandparents, siblings, and in-laws, just like these Israelite tribes had their people, you guys are our people—and I'm just so grateful God gave us you.

Kara, my publisher, thanks for taking the risk to take me on. You made my big dream come true, and in turn, you got to try Minnesota's best deep-dish pizza. I think it was a win-win?

Donna, my editor, my husband always knew when you emailed me because my knee-jerk reaction was to yell, "I JUST LOVE MY EDITOR." I just couldn't help myself! You made my least favorite part of this book-writing process a *breeze*, and I hope I'm paired with you forevermore. (But seriously, Kara, please make this happen.)

My whole Tyndale team, thanks (x *infinity*) for inviting me once again to partner with you in the mission to share God's Word in a way people can relate to and *understand*. Cheering you on forever.

My social media friends, you know who you are. Maybe you go all the way back to Bachelor Rants. Maybe you helped name our baby Dottie by a viral reel. Or maybe you saw me spit my food out because I forgot to pray first. However we crossed paths, know that from the bottom of my heart I'm so glad we did. God is on the move—online and in person—and let's keep putting Him on display, yeah? See you on the gram . . .

About the Author

HEIDI LEE ANDERSON is the author of *P.S. It's Gonna Be Good*, a speaker, and a stay-at-home mom. While crafting devotionals for hundreds of thousands of followers on social media @heidileeanderson and @thismotherhen, she's a master at cleaning up Cheerio spills and building LEGO towers while simultaneously chugging coffee like a Gilmore. Heidi has spent her career doing ministry—from teaching hundreds in kids' ministry to writing daily devotionals, Bible reading plans, and small group curriculum as a content developer for adults. After being diagnosed with cancer, Heidi's fuel is now to make sure that Christ-followers realize, know, and claim the sure promises God offers—in the mundane, amid the heartache, and on top of the highest mountains.

Also from Tyndale House Publishers

Available at Tyndale.com or wherever books are sold!

CP1970